A
FOOTBALL
STORY

PETER F.
LESTER

Published in the United States of America

Brilliant Books Literary
137 Forest Park Lane Thomasville
North Carolina 27360 USA

ISBN
Paperback: 979-8-88945-295-9
Ebook: 979-8-88945-296-6

ACKNOWLEDGEMENTS

Comments and constructive criticisms from my Kona Writing Group and preliminary editing by Linda Lapka were key inputs in the completion of *A Football Story*. The book could not have been completed without the inspiration of my wife, Julia Beebe Lester, and my daughters, Heather Lester and Rachael Lester Posada.

1.

A cold wind shook the last leaves of autumn from the white oaks surrounding Western Kansas University's packed Arnold Stadium. Light snowflakes randomly decorated hats and jackets of the excited spectators standing to loudly welcome the WKU Prairie Dogs and the Mammoths of Michigan College as they jogged onto the field for their pregame warmups. The players were escorted by lively cheerleaders, who defied the chilly temperatures in their brief outfits, more suited for the first game of the season three months ago.

Today was the final regular-season game. It was a big one. Both teams were undefeated. The winner would be the conference champion with an invitation to the national playoffs. The importance of the contest was reflected in the crowd of media people crammed into the press box. Sportswriters from the local newspaper the *Argyle Record* were joined by reporters from Kansas City, Omaha, Denver, and Chicago. Their binoculars, phones, and laptop computers were strewn across the table below the broad window that gave a spectacular view of the field. The kickoff was only a few minutes away.

The matchup would be a major turning point for these two strong squads. The week leading up to the game had kept sports commentators busy in anticipation of the face-off. Both teams had just missed the playoffs the previous season. This year, things were much different. The two squads were undefeated. Local and national press opinions agreed: this game was a toss-up.

Crowd noise outside the press box continued to rise in anticipation of the kickoff. Josh White, a reporter from the *Kansas City Star*, raised his voice above the chatter, "Hey, people, let's face it—the real difference in this game is WKU's Mike Wolf. Believe me, this game will turn on his play! There is no doubt that he'll be a first-round NFL draftee when he's done at WKU."

Both teams had outstanding players, but the Prairie Dogs' senior halfback Mike Wolf had devastated WKU, rushing and scoring records with his performances during this season. At six feet and 210 pounds, he was not only fast, but his pass-catching ability was, in a word, amazing. A recent news article had aptly labeled him Sticky-Hands Wolf.

Another sportswriter commented, "I've heard that several proscouts have already made informal contacts with him. There's no doubt in my mind that there will be more of them knocking on his door to offer him contracts. I wonder who will grab him?" He laughed. "You can bet there will be some big bucks changing hands!"

Buck Jones, a well-known Kansas City TV sports commentator, shook his head. "We can't be so sure. I do agree, the pros are certainly eyeing him, but exactly when he will join a professional team is the hanging question. I've heard that he still has at least a year of classes before he can graduate. We're just going to have to wait and see."

Wolf was certainly a senior in the number of college credits he had completed, but those were not the ones he needed for a degree. They were just a number that he needed to stay eligible.

There was laughter in the response to the reporter's remark. A voice at the crowded window exclaimed, "C'mon! This is college football. You don't think that Wolf will refuse a gazillion-dollar contract to finish a degree, do you? I've spoken with him several times on just that topic. My takeaway is that classes aren't his favorite thing—it's football!' He chuckled. "Make that football and girls!"

Rachel Rich, a well-known reporter from a local TV station, stood at corner of the press box with her arms crossed. She smiled at the remark. "Girls aside, I agree, Wolf is good, but as far as this game goes, he's going to need some great play by the rest of his team. I'm not going to write off the Mammoths—not quite yet. They might not have a star like Wolf, but their team dynamic is something to behold. Coach Mayfield has a squad that works together in a way I haven't seen in a long time. We're lucky to be here. You can bet that it's going to be a great game!"

At the sound of the referee's whistle, the conversations in the press box came to an end. All attention was focused on the kickoff.

Just a few minutes into the first quarter, the Mammoths scored. They followed that with a surprise for the Prairie Dogs—a fake kick and a two- point conversion. Six minutes later, Mike Wolf made a spectacular run around left end and outsprinted the defense for a WKU touchdown. But the Dogs' attempt to match the Mammoths' earlier score with their own two-point conversion was not to be. A long pass across the field was tipped away from Wolf's outstretched hands by a defensive back. At the end of the half, the score remained 8-6, in favor of the Mammoths.

Ralph Schwartz was a history professor, in his twelfth year as a faculty member at WKU. A giant of a man, his build revealed his football past. Although his alma mater was UCLA, he and his wife, Virginia, had been Prairie Dog fans as long as they had been on campus. Today, they were happy to have great seats on the forty-yard line.

In Ralph's mind, the Prairie Dogs could do no wrong. Virginia glanced at him during a break in the play. She laughed and shook her head at her husband's intense interest in every aspect of the game. "Ralph, if we have been to one of these games, we have been to fifty. I claim long experience in watching you watch them! I think you may be infected. Can you tell me, does this 'football disease' ever go away?"

Ralph laughed at her question. "Are you kidding? I'll be here until I fall down the stadium steps!"

She rolled her eyes with an ironic smile. "I guess I have always known that, but now and then, I have to verify that that problem—that football condition—still lurks in your head."

Ralph sat back with a grin. "Ah, my love, I do have to admit that you have to put up with my football mentality. I am forever thankful for your patience, especially at this time of year."

Virginia glanced up at the jammed press box and then scanned the stadium to see a dozen or more TV cameras at strategic locations. The attention-grabbing commercial advertisements posted around the stadium were hard to miss. Big-time football was in the air.

She turned to her husband. "Ralph, for some reason, WKU football seems to be a little different this year. What's up?"

He glanced at the scoreboard, thoughtfully rubbing his chin. "You're right, Ginny, this year is different. The Prairie Dogs have a terrific chance to go big. We could win the conference championship and go to the nationals. What a concept! The WKU Prairie Dogs from out here in the boonies of the high plains playing the big guys—winning the national championship is not a fantasy anymore. We have the horses. We can do it!" She smiled at his enthusiasm and gave her own analysis, "Ralph, to me, there is more to it than just having a good chance in the playoffs—it seems that the whole football program at WKU is a little different this season." Ralph looked over at her. "Different? How? Yeah, players and coaches come and go, but it's still football—eleven players on each side, a hundred yards between goal lines, four downs. Still good old American football.

What's your point?"

Virginia shook her head, wrinkling her brow. "I'm not sure that I can really explain it. Maybe it's the teams, the crowd, the media, or the ads. Probably all of them. It's just that, more and more, it seems to me that football operates more like a business on campus—something separate from the academic side." She shook her head. "Look at that ad on the wall above the fifty-yard line." She read it out loud, "Real football fans drink Buffalo Beer."

Ralph was silent. He had heard her clearly, but he kept his eyes on the field. Virginia's comment was an awkward distraction as the teams lined up for the second half kickoff. They stood with the rest of the crowd, enveloped by the enthusiastic clamor in anticipation of the kickoff. He leaned over to her. "Ginny, you make some good points about a complicated problem, but it's a little too noisy here for a serious discussion. Why don't we continue after the game?"

The third quarter brought some spectacular passes and runs by both teams, but the score did not change. Mike Wolf gave WKU an instant of hope when he caught a short pass on the 25 and sprinted down the sideline. He was hit at the four-yard line but still managed to fall into the end zone, dragging a tackler with him. The loud celebration by his teammates and WKU fans was short-lived. Wolf had stepped out of bounds on the eighteen-yard line. A first down but no touchdown.

Three downs later, they had gained only four yards. The next play, the Dogs faked a field goal and attempted a long pass. Unfortunately, a Mammoths' linebacker dove through a gap next to the center and managed to deflect the ball just as it left the quarterback's hand. The score remained in the Mammoths' favor: 8-6.

The scoreless back-and-forth play continued for nearly the entire fourth quarter. With only a few minutes to go, the Mammoths took the ball to the WKU 40, where the Prairie Dogs held them for four downs and took back possession. Just twenty-five seconds on the clock. Two spectacular pass plays carried the Prairie Dogs to their opponents' nine-yard line. A time-out stopped the clock with three seconds left.

Fourth down. One last play—the difference between winning and losing the game and the conference championship. A thunderous roar enveloped the stadium as the Dogs' quarterback shouted a play into the faces of his team gathered around him.

The huddle broke. Mike Wolf trotted out to the left flank. At the snap of the ball, he brush-blocked the defensive end and sprinted downfield. The quarterback faked right then turned and fired a low pass to Wolf, who made a spectacular juggling catch at the five. He sprinted for the goal line, where two defensive backs racing from opposite sides of the field hammered him to the ground.

Mike's only memory of that long-ago game was the unearthly crack of his right leg. He never heard the crowd's thunderous celebration as he fell into the end zone and hit the ground with the ball clutched in his arms. No, his reality was opening his eyes in a hospital room twenty-four hours later to realize that, for him, football was no more.

2.

Early on an August morning, Mike Wolf left his newly rented apartment and walked quickly onto the campus of Western Kansas University. His visit for a job interview just a few months earlier had brought him an offer as an assistant professor in engineering. He took it.

His walk across the university grounds gave him the distinct feeling of being home. He knew this place. Directly ahead of him rose the iconic symbol of WKU, a tall brick fortress known as Tower Hall, the oldest building on campus. Just to his left was the Miller Hall of Science, a reminder of his postfootball academic struggles to reinvent himself as a serious student.

The university grounds had retained their park-like aspect during his absence. Many trees and wide grassy areas surrounded the sidewalks between buildings. Except for a few maintenance trucks and shuttle buses, vehicles were relegated to the periphery of the campus. Mike smiled at the thought of being back in WKU walking environment. *Students come here to learn and faculty come to teach—whatever the results of those efforts, simply moving between classes caused most of them to end up in better physical shape. For Mike, it was certainly good exercise for his bum leg.*

A light morning breeze brushed over Mike. It carried the scent of recently mown grass from Arnold Stadium on the north side of the campus. He could hear the yells of football coaches and players busy with a preseason practice. Until this moment, he thought that his long efforts in grad school had erased what he called his football genes. Not so—the noise of the practice was enough to produce a surge of that old pregame adrenaline.

A pleasant-looking guy with brown eyes and a friendly smile, Mike Wolf's curly black hair danced over his forehead in the gentle breeze. He carried his six-foot frame well. Even at a lighter 180 pounds, despite his limp, Mike still looked like he could step onto a football field and make a difference. He shook his head at the memories. It seemed like it was yesterday when he was out there running, catching, blocking, and tackling. Mike's broken leg had changed everything. He dropped out of WKU and moved back home—a small town near the Texas Gulf Coast. He picked up a job at a local minimart, something he had done as a high school student. Otherwise, his life involved mostly drinking beer and sleeping—losing touch with his college friends.

Then, one long summer weekend, his dad took him fishing on Arnie's Bayou, a short walk from home. Relaxing hours talking, tying flies, casting, and trolling quietly had a positive effect on Mike. One bright morning, the stress from his football injury was gone. Mike relaxed. His dad even noticed the change.

An electrical engineer, his father took advantage of those stress-free hours to gently remind Mike that he had been a better-than-average high school student with a clear talent in math and science. He didn't push his son; he just suggested a new direction.

Mike finally realized that, yes, there was life after football. A few weeks later, he brought his new attitude to a local junior college to make up some failed WKU classes and to take some new math and physics courses. After a year, he was back at WKU as a requalified and determined undergraduate student. He followed in his father's footsteps, transferring hard work and desire for success to the study of computer science, leaning toward engineering.

It wasn't easy. He spent hours at his books—in class—at the computer. Although he probably didn't make the connection, it was clear to anyone who knew him that his focus and determination on the football field now came through in his academic efforts. On those occasions when he got his nose academically bloodied, he knew exactly what to do: get up, huddle up, get out there, and hit harder.

Mike showed more than a good brain as a reborn student. In three years, his positive attitude and hard work paid off with a bachelor's degree in computer science from WKU and an assistantship in the graduate program in computer engineering at the University of Illinois. Six years later and he was back at WKU with a PhD, hired as an assistant professor.

On the day of his return, his walk across campus reminded him of the beauty of the grounds of WKU. There had been some obvious changes, attesting to the growth of the school during his absence. An impressive new library building now stood as a response to the digitization phenomena that swept through all universities. Still a repository of books on paper, the library now gave rapid access to electronic books, data, and other information stored both on campus and out in the ether. Mike's engineering students would make good use of that facility.

Besides the new buildings, he noticed something different about the look of older halls and classroom buildings he had known so well in his undergraduate days. Stopping to study the sight, it finally dawned on him. The cottonwoods and elms that dotted the campus were taller and fuller, shading otherwise familiar corners, entrances, and windows of those structures. He shook his head at the amount of time—almost ten years now—that had flown by since his football disaster. Mike laughed at himself. *Yeah, we're all a bit older.*

3.

Mike glanced at his watch. Jet-lagged and early for a meeting with his department chairman, he detoured to the faculty cafeteria with an appetite for breakfast.

A short time later, he carried a tray loaded with waffles, syrup, toast, jam, and coffee toward an empty table when he was distracted by a shout from across the room. He glanced to his right, searching for the source. No one he knew. Too late, he was face-to-face with a young woman carrying her own loaded tray. Their collision was accompanied by the noisy scattering of silverware, broken dishes, and glassware across the floor.

The low hum of conversations was suddenly replaced by a brief silence with people jumping to their feet with exclamations of "Uh-oh!" "Oh no!" and "Whoops!"

The chatter across the room gradually resumed with head-shaking and stifled laughter as the incident was comprehensively analyzed as only college professors can analyze.

Neither of the two involved in the collision was laughing. Mike winced, shaking his head at the jumble of food on the floor. He looked up at his cohort in mess-making. A slender young woman with her briefcase under her arm and her breakfast tray at her feet—she glared at him. Her face burned with embarrassment as she stomped her feet to shake crumbs from her sandals.

They backed away from the remnants of food and drinks spread across the floor. She continued to stare darts at Mike as student waiters arrived with brooms and mops. Mike made one apology after another. "I'm really sorry. I wasn't watching where I was going and . . ." Shaking his head, he said sheepishly, "Damn, I'm sorry. Are you OK?"

She was silent. Head down, shoulders slumping, her hands hung at her sides as she watched spilled coffee and syrup spread down the front of her dress. She took a deep breath and looked up at Mike with a hint of a smile. "Well, I guess this is one way for a new faculty member to get herself noticed."

Mike grabbed a fallen napkin to brush syrup and crumbs off his clothes, saying with a sigh, "Make that *two* new faculty members."

"I'm Laura Sparks." She started to offer Mike her hand but pulled it back with a grimace. "I think I'm a bit too sticky to be shaking hands."

"I'm Mike Wolf, Laura. Can I buy you a . . ." he hesitated, searching for the right words, "a breakfast do-over?"

Laura looked down at the darkening stains that were a greasy contrast to the blue of her dress. She wrinkled her nose, shaking her head at his proposal. "Thanks, but I don't think I am quite dressed for the occasion." He stepped back to assess the damage to her clothes. "Can I at least walk with you back to wherever you are going? I could share some of the embarrassment. Anyway, it doesn't look that bad."

Laura laughed as she grabbed a handful of paper napkins to wipe the mess off her clothes. She finally shook her head at her failed effort and looked back at Mike. "Well—despite your flawed opinion of my clothing— sure, let's go."

They didn't pay attention to the titters of other faculty as they stepped out of the cafeteria into the pleasant morning air. Mike looked closely at his companion. Short blond hair and brown eyes—a slim five foot seven or so. He guessed that athletics had been part of her background. An old potential-date assessment technique kicked in. *Hmmm, no ring.*

A warm breeze followed them across a bridge over the stream that marked the eastern boundary of the campus. The trees along the edge of the water provided mottled shade from the morning sun.

Although they had just met and probably neither of them could explain the reason, Laura and Mike were aware of an easy link between them, something more than the fact that they were both new faculty members. Their conversation was light and curious.

Perhaps it was Mike's laugh and self-effacing manner that relaxed her.

She noticed that he limped slightly. "What's your field, Michael?" "Computer engineering. You?"

"Biology. Marine biology. Where did you do your graduate work?" "University of Illinois. What was your path to this place?"

Mike could hear her enthusiasm as she described her academic road. "Undergrad at UNC. Biology. I did my graduate work in marine biology at the University of Miami."

He scratched his head. "What's a marine biologist doing at this landlocked place?"

"I guess it does seem odd at first. Yes, here in Kansas, I'm a long way from the beach!

"There has been a long relationship between Western Kansas University and the University of Miami. Many WKU biology grad students are involved in oceanographic studies off the Florida Coast. In fact, those students were my initial contacts with this place.

"Seven months ago, I saw an ad for a WKU faculty position in marine biology in one of my journals. I applied and was brought out for an interview and to give a seminar on my dissertation work. That led to an invitation to apply for a faculty position, and a few weeks later, I had an offer. It was that quick! I also had a couple of others—one on the West Coast and another in Maine. But I decided this place offered the best opportunities to teach and maintain my connections in Florida."

They continued to enjoy each other's company as they walked the few blocks to Laura's apartment. There was a pause in their conversation as they strolled in the pleasant morning air. Mike was processing the fact that this was the first time in months that he had had an opportunity to simply chat with a single woman outside the classroom. If he could have read her mind, he would have known that Laura was having similar thoughts about him. They turned to face each other at the door of her apartment. For a few seconds, both experienced an unstated wish to continue. Then Laura gently reminded him of her need to change her clothes and continue her class preparations.

Mike glanced at his watch. "Uh-oh! I had better get moving myself. I have a meeting with my department chairman in ten minutes. No doubt he will have some choice words of wisdom for me. Late is not an option!"

Stepping off the porch, Mike smiled warmly and waved to Laura. "I owe you a breakfast."

Laura found herself laughing easily with her new friend. "A good idea, Michael! Why don't we try the cafeteria again? Perhaps a little more gracefully next time."

Mike laughed. "I'll call!"

4.

Ten minutes later, the secretary of the Computer Engineering Department escorted Mike into the chairman's spacious office, where Ed Johnson greeted him with a broad smile and a firm handshake.

Professor Johnson was not on the faculty when Mike was an undergraduate. Their only previous face-to-face meeting had been during Mike's job interview a few months ago. Prior to that encounter, he had reviewed his new boss's impressive resume on the WKU website. More than just a good department chairman, Johnson's opinions were often sought by those dealing with the broader issues of university business. A talented manager, he still found time to teach and to advise students while keeping a hand in his research specialty, wind-power engineering. Mike was pleased to have this man as his boss.

He barely sat down when Johnson's dominating presence took over. Only about five feet, six inches with a slight build, he was constantly in motion. Mike would soon learn that Professor Johnson's intense, peripatetic behavior was not unusual. He was well-known for teaching classes and conducting meetings on his feet. Today was no exception. He paced back and forth behind his desk, gesticulating with every important point he made—and there were many.

An hour later, on his chair's recommendation, Mike visited other offices for introductions to department personnel. Despite a bit of information overload, the sincere welcoming attitude of everyone made him comfortable as a new member of the faculty.

He did notice that there was greater formality in the comments of a few of the older professors who were here when he completed his undergraduate work in engineering.

Their demeanor reminded him of his experiences with them as a student. That aspect of their collegiality needed time to become more relaxed.

Mike winced as he ascended the stairs of the engineering building to inspect his own office on the fourth floor. His leg had never been quite right after the ugliness of the break in that last football game, and it especially protested stair-climbing. The four stairwells on the way to his office were on the edge of his comfort zone, prompting a stop on each level for a brief rest. He could have used the elevator—he just hated to wait for it. Although his doctor had doubted it, Mike argued with himself that climbing would strengthen his leg. "No pain, no gain!" He had to laugh at that cliché—it was right on.

His office mate Jerry Larson greeted Mike at the door of their office. They shook hands as Mike looked around at his "new and roomy" work space. He had hoped for something better than what he had as a graduate student. That description was a stretch for this place. At best, it could be described as a very old one-professor office for two professors.

There was a distinct army surplus aspect to the worn furniture. The windowless hall-like space was filled on one side with two gray metal desks, chairs, a couple of tall shelves, and two filing cabinets. On the opposite wall, a coatrack in one corner kept company with a long table that overflowed with computers, printers, and displays. At least the computer equipment seemed to be up-to-date.

"Hi, Jerry, I'm Mike Wolf. It looks like the last thing you need in here is a roommate!"

At thirty-two, Jerry was a tall, lanky guy. About six feet four, his slight downward look at Mike, coupled with his neatly combed dark hair and sharp jaw, gave the impression of a no-nonsense military type. That perception disappeared immediately when they shook hands.

Jerry agreed with Mike's comment as he watched his new officemate inspect his cramped work space. "Welcome to life as a new assistant prof. I've been here a year." He laughed. "When I arrived, they told me that a larger office was in the works—whatever that meant."

Reminding Jerry that he had just left graduate school where space often meant nearly sitting on top of each other, Mike assured his new office mate that he could deal with the tight quarters.

"Mike, I welcome your company. I attended your seminar when you were here for your interview last spring. Good stuff. We'll have some common interests to kick around."

"Thanks, Jerry. It certainly is good to be here with grad school behind me—finally! I have to admit that there were times when I thought I'd never get back here." He smiled. "Now, I almost can't believe it. I'm still on a high!"

Jerry watched Mike inspect his desk, opening and closing drawers, planning the organization of bookcases, file cabinets, and computer equipment. "You know, Mike, being a graduate of this university and this particular department puts you in a unique position. You are familiar with this place. That is really an advantage. Sure, some of your former instructors will still see that Mike Wolf, Student sign on your forehead, but I have a feeling that all that stuff will go away pretty fast."

Mike was already feeling comfortable in his office, despite the close quarters. Jerry's presence and sense of humor helped relax him. He sat down and spread his hands out on his new . . . old desk. "So far so good!" He was pleased to share an office with a friendly, slightly more experienced fellow newbie. Mike received some good practical advice from Jerry about everything, from dealing with their department chair and other senior professors to scheduling.

"Oh yeah, I almost forgot one more thing. In case you are ready to hunker down on those ever-so-light course preparations, student advisement, and your wind-power studies." He laughed. "Be ready for something more—something grad school doesn't exactly prepare you for."

Mike was curious. He chuckled. "More? In this tight place, I don't think there's room for more."

Jerry rubbed his hands together. "There is a well-known truism that covers another responsibility that you have just taken on." He laughed at the thought. "As the old saw goes, *in a university, there are no great professors, there are only great committees.*

"The university runs on committees: curriculum committees, budget committees, committees to advise our higher-ups, committees to oversee student activities, award committees, and on and on. Everybody does committee work. You will participate, sooner or later.

"Fortunately, new faculty usually begin slowly with only a couple of assignments—far as I'm concerned, it's not slow enough. I've only been here a year, and I am already on three departmental committees—plus the library advisory committee. From what I've seen, some committees are useless, but most are important for the health of both the department and the university."

He turned back to the work on his desk and smiled. "Enough academic orientation! You need to get yourself organized. Don't let me distract you. "Oh yeah, I almost forgot. There is one more thing. The general faculty meeting to kick off the academic year will be in the main auditorium next Friday at one p.m. The higher-ups, including the president, tell us what's coming. It's usually informative and, thankfully, relatively short. Why don't we meet here, say at twelve thirty, and go over together?"

Mike pulled up his smartphone to make another note, nodding. "You're on, Jerry! I'll be here."

5.

Mike's days leading up to the beginning of the semester were full: class preparations, engineering faculty meetings, and new committee assignments. He was now a member of both the curriculum and graduate committees and an adviser for freshman engineering students. Student visits to his office increased as fall semester approached.

Those activities seemed small compared to his lecture and lab preparations. There were a couple of easy freshman courses including Introduction to Software Engineering, a broad review of the field for new students. But then there were his specialties, *Digital Design* and *Computer Networks*. He knew the material but now he had to put himself in the instructor's shoes or, as he thought of it, *to be on the other end of the stick.*

A couple of new graduate students had dropped in to chat with him, curious about his specialty, wind-energy prospecting. That research had not yet gotten beyond his desk, but he was well-funded on a couple of recent grants to begin his fieldwork. Good graduate students were key to moving those projects along. He interviewed several, finding one that not only had the interest but also possessed some useful background in fieldwork.

Preparations spilled over from his office to his apartment. Nights seemed too short. He was glued to his computer screen well after midnight, reviewing course material and preparing online assignments and study guides. Classes and labs weren't his only concerns. Support for his research work required him to spend hours preparing successful proposals for outside funding.

Empty takeout bags, used napkins, and paper plates were scattered around his kitchen table and filled the trash can. Only when they began to spill onto the floor did he declare a time-out to clean up the mess.

Mike thought he had known what he was getting into, but there was just not enough time. It seemed that his clock had only two critical hours on it: 6:00 a.m., time to get up and get at it, and 1:00 a.m., time to fall into bed. Even so, he found the process exciting. He was tired but very happy to be at WKU.

One warm afternoon, just a few days before the start of the semester, he took a break and walked across campus to sit for a half hour in the nearly empty stands of Arnold Stadium. The Prairie Dogs were busy with an afternoon practice getting ready for the first game of the season.

He leaned back on the empty bench behind him, automatically shifting into his football mind-set. He quickly focused not only on the individual players but also on play execution and coach-player interactions. The team looked sharp. He noticed a halfback who was exceptionally fast and displayed an amazing ability to change direction at full speed, leaving defensive backs stumbling after him. Mike looked over at another spectator sitting a few empty rows away and asked who that player was.

"Ray Smith. Probably our best bet for All-American—quite an athlete." Mike had to agree, Smith looked very good.

Mike's love for football had never really gone away after his injury and his departure from the playing field so many seasons ago. Even with the demands of his new position, he had managed to squeeze in a few quarters of early season football on TV. Today, twenty minutes in the WKU stadium watching the Prairie Dogs' practice was very special. This was the stadium where he had played. He felt that he was back—reconnected to his team and their game.

Mike and Jerry Larson walked across campus to the general faculty meeting. It was a great early September day—warm, not a cloud in the sky. Jerry glanced at his office mate. "Mike, you look a tad worn out."

Mike nodded, giving a weary smile at Jerry's observation. "I suppose I am." He laughed. "I have been spending a lot of time in that head-down, butt-up position that football players and new assistant professors know so well."

Jerry gave Mike a pat on the back. "Don't worry, we've all staggered through a first semester. Look at it as an initiation. From what I've seen, you're doing fine. Just things will get better."

Mike smiled ironically, shrugging his shoulders. "Thanks, Jerry. I'm really OK. I can't afford to be worried. There's not enough time for that." A block from the main campus auditorium, they passed a groundskeeper intent on raking the lawn. It was hard to miss him. The rake looked like a dinner fork in his hands. He was tall—at least six feet eight. His blue jeans were supported by suspenders stretched over a plaid shirt that barely covered his enormous belly. Mike pointed to him. "Now there's a big guy!

I bet he played—"

He stopped abruptly. "Jerry, I think I know him! That's Joe Kozlowski! I played football with him a long time ago! Still a big guy. We called him Tank. Give me a minute. I'll catch up with you."

Mike stepped off the sidewalk and approached his old friend. A few feet away, he called out, "Hey, Tank! Haven't seen you for too long. How's it going?"

Tank stopped raking and looked up, wrinkling his brow as he slowly answered, "Hi. My name is Joe. What is your name?"

Mike was shocked by the slow drawl. Tank seemed disconnected, almost lost. "Tank, it's me, Mike Wolf! You and I played together—you were my favorite blocker! Now here we are, together again, both back at old Kansas Western!"

A dim light went on in Tank's eyes. He smiled crookedly with a hint of recognition. "Mike? Yeah . . . football. Sorry, I don't 'zactly remember . . . but I sorta do."

They awkwardly shook hands, then Mike asked how long Tank had been working at the university.

He hesitated, finally drawling out an answer. "Hmm . . . not sure . . . a long time ago, I had some hard head bumps in some games and . . . it was . . . it was . . ."

Closing his eyes, Tank tapped his forehead with his thick fingers. "I didn't remember stuff. I didn't play anymore football . . . didn't play. I didn't go to school anymore . . . wasn't sure what to do."

Then, a random memory bank suddenly opened, and Tank grinned and nodded. "Coach Anderson helped me find this job. I like it."

Mike responded, "Tank, I just started working here at the university. I guess we'll see each other now and then. Do you work here all the time?"

Flattered by the attention, Tank grinned. "Yeah, I rake leaves now . . . and pull weeds. I shovel snow when it gets cold."

Mike realized he was nearly late for the general faculty meeting. "Tank, I have to go. Let's talk again. Where do you live?"

"Well . . . ahh . . . the bus takes me home in the afternoon . . . takes me home. I have a room with some buddies. We eat downstairs and watch TV. I like it."

Mike put a hand on Tank's shoulder. "I'll find it, and I'll come to see you again. We can talk some more." Another crooked smile creased Tank's face. "Sure . . . OK . . . bye."

Mike waved back at Tank and walked slowly toward the faculty meeting. There was a time when Tank was a tremendous football player with a personality as big as his body. He told great jokes, laughed at life, and chased girls with the rest of his buddies. Yeah, he goofed off when it came to classes, but he was smart— just more interested in football. Mike recalled a long-ago discussion he and Tank had about politics. It was during a national election. Mike had been amazed at Tank's knowledge of the issues and where he stood. There was no question about Tank having a good mind. That Tank was gone.

Mike shook his head. It was as if he was trying to help clear the cobwebs from his own brain. *What a crappy situation! I'm not even sure he really recognized me. It's like he's been wasted!*

6.

few minutes later, Mike caught up with his office mate at the door of the auditorium. They hurried into the general faculty meeting and grabbed a couple of seats just as the crowd was quieting down.

This meeting, always held in the main campus auditorium on the Friday before fall classes began, was typically an upbeat beginning for the academic year. The president, Jane Summerville, spoke first. In her early sixties, she was a large woman with a pleasant and self-assured manner. Despite the hot September day, she wore a light-green long-sleeved business suit. Her neat gray hair fell just below her ears. An exclamation point to her attire was the pair of reading glasses that sat precariously on the end of her nose. A glance at her face told you who was in charge.

Summerville began by asking all new faculty members to stand. With a welcoming smile, she led the applause that greeted them. Mike enjoyed the moment as he stood with the group. He looked around to see Laura on her feet just a few rows behind him. They waved to each other, and their eyes met for a second. Mike again sensed an undefinable connection with her, something beyond academics. He shook his head with at the thought. *C'mon, Mike, back to business!*

The president introduced some special guests and recognized several faculty members who had had outstanding academic successes in the past year. Her well-organized and informative presentation was completed with a summary of critical changes in the annual budget and a report on the state of important construction projects on campus. A week earlier, Mike had met President Summerville at a welcome luncheon for new faculty members. Then and now, she displayed a wide knowledge of university business and management and demonstrated a remarkable ability to clearly explain some quite complicated issues.

After a standing applause, President Summerville turned the podium over to the Athletics director, Tim Barnes. He summarized last year's performances by women's and men's teams, noting the high finishes in their respective leagues. Two nationally ranked wrestlers and a hammer thrower from WKU's outstanding track team were asked to rise to receive standing ovations.

Finally, the head football coach, Mitch Anderson, came forward to discuss the upcoming football season. Welcomed by a loud ovation, everyone in the audience anticipated the beginning of what everyone knew could be a national championship season. The first football game was only a day away, and excitement was in the air.

Barnes responded to the crowd, raising his arms and shouting, "Western Kansas University Prairie Dogs rule!" Many in the crowd stood and applauded, noisily showing their support.

Barnes and Anderson took turns praising the team. There was much to be proud of; WKU's football team was one of the better teams in the league. Since Mike's days, it had won the league championship two more times and barely missed on three other occasions, including last year. Coach Anderson assured the audience that this year was going to be different. He reviewed the schedule for the upcoming season and the status of this year's team. He was confident of WKU's chances to reach to the playoffs. He closed his presentation with a loud "Go Dogs!" He and the Athletics director left the stage as the auditorium filled with noisy cheers and traditional Prairie Dog barks.

This was the first time that Mike had seen his old coach since he had returned to WKU. Watching Anderson brought back many old memories of football practices and games. The coach was good at what he did, not only in bringing out the best in his players but also in stoking fan support. Mike smiled at

Anderson's familiar enthusiasm, making a mental note to visit him in the next few weeks.

A few minutes later, Jerry and Mike followed the dispersing crowd out of the hall. Mike was chatting happily about the excitement of the meeting when he saw Laura in the distance making her way to another exit. Just about to disappear through the door, she looked back for a brief second, and she and Mike made eye contact, smiling and waving to each other.

Mike and Jerry stepped outside into a pleasant late summer day. Mike was happy with the enthusiastic start for the semester and the renewal of his old connection to football. He clapped his hands and smiled as that enthusiasm spilled out. "Yep, Jerry! This is my university! My team! I am home!"

Mike spent the next day back in his apartment, alternating between preparations for his first classes and watching the Prairie Dogs on TV. They handled the away game easily—bringing home a 35-10 victory. He realized that his return to WKU and, especially, watching his first Dogs' game in a long time had reactivated what he called his football genes.

After the end of the game, he focused on the start of classes on the following Monday. He was responsible for two lectures and three labs per week plus regular online interactions and occasional office visits with students. He knew this hectic schedule was coming since he was hired. Now he was in it—and it was even busier than he had anticipated. His preparations were a major part of his home time, as he called his long evening hours the chair at his desk--the kitchen table. Late that evening, he read himself to sleep with a copy of the current Prairie Dogs' football roster.

7.

Mike walked slowly toward his apartment. He squinted his eyes at the sun sinking toward the horizon—a reminder of another long day in his first semester as a new faculty member. His limp was more noticeable late in the afternoon. He stopped beside a bench to do a couple of stretches. They only made the ache worse. He was determined—sooner or later—to get himself into better shape.

Despite his busy days in the classroom and labs, he finally managed a few visits to the gym. There was an unanticipated benefit of those brief workouts. He met several WKU athletes. Given his new position in the Athletics Board, he was pleased with that opportunity. Since football season was underway and those players spent most of their workout time on field, those he encountered in the gym were mainly from baseball, basketball, and track-and-field, involved in off-season strength training. Mike quickly discovered that they were not without opinions about football.

A couple of athletes were unusually negative. "Those football guys are treated like gold," one discus thrower noted. "We work as hard or harder on our fitness and practice. We are good, but we never get much notice compared to the Dogs' football players. The school paper, the local sports pundits—no, they're not interested in anything else but big-time football." Mike had never given much thought to the higher priority of WKU football over other sports. He tried to imagine himself on the track team—working hard to represent WKU but with minimal recognition.

He pushed his football thoughts to another place, mentally reviewing his classes. He had no doubts about his labs. He was comfortable with hands-on work; he knew the material and especially enjoyed his computer design lab. On the other hand, his lectures needed some tweaking. He was not yet comfortable in that mode, and his students sensed it. His slides were too busy, causing some eyes to glaze over. And he needed a better review of the notes on his iPad before each lecture.

Mike laughed at himself. *More work to do!* Academic stresses he had suffered as a student seemed pretty innocuous now. Being on the other end of the academic stick certainly demanded more energy than he had realized.

He pushed his pace despite the ache. He had a busy evening of preparation ahead. Suddenly, he was startled by a familiar voice. "Hey, I know you!"

Mike looked up to see his former football coach Mitch Anderson. Quickly stifling the word *Coach*, so automatic in his previous role as a team member, he responded, "Mitch! Great to see you."

They shook hands and gave each other friendly pats on the shoulders as Mike said, "I've followed the Prairie Dogs ever since I left WKU. What a record. I caught your presentation at the general faculty meeting. Can't wait for our first home game."

Anderson's hair was bit grayer than during Mike's playing days, yet at a slim six feet two, he still possessed the build of an athlete and the stature of a head coach.

He was obviously pleased with their meeting. "Mike, it's been way too long. I remember your graduation. We were all proud of you for sticking with academics to finish your degree after that god-awful leg injury. What in the world are you doing back here?"

Mike shook his head with a bit of a grimace at the memory. "Thankfully, those dark days of casts and physical therapy were long ago. Things got better. After I finally finished my BS degree here at WKU, grad school at University of Illinois was my focus. Matter of fact, I've just been hired back here as an assistant professor."

Mitch was astonished. "Wow! You, the jock of the past—a professor!

I'll be damned! What department?"

"Computer engineering. Now I am learning to teach, move my research along, and do whatever else it takes. Sometimes it's a bit overwhelming. I only hope my students aren't suffering."

Anderson chuckled. "Knowing you, I bet they aren't. By the way, Mike, with your connection to the team, I will be happy to give you some prime seats for our home games. In fact, if you want to sit on the bench with the players, just let me know."

Mike shook his head. "Thanks for the offer, Mitch, but I think I'll skip the bench." He grinned. "I already know what sweat smells like. But a good seat in the stands would be great."

Anderson nodded. "Consider it done. Just drop by my office, and I'll take care of you. By the way, you look like you're still in good shape."

"Thanks, Mitch. I'm doing OK. Walking back and forth across campus is good for me. Now and then I even get to the gym for a workout. I'm good."

Mitch glanced at the clock on Tower Hall. "I've got a meeting with some visiting high school athletes in about thirty minutes. I'd better go. Give me a call, Mike. Let's talk again over a cup of coffee."

After a warm handshake, Anderson began to walk back to his office. Suddenly, he snapped his fingers and shouted, "Hey, Mike, hang on! I just realized that there is a great way for you to help the team. Let's talk for another minute."

Mike turned back toward Anderson with a smile. "Sure, Coach, just as long as I don't have to step on the field."

The late afternoon sun was a giant orange ball when Mike and Mitch Anderson walked over to a shaded bench between campus buildings. The seat was low, and Mike sat down awkwardly, pushing his stiff leg out in front of him. Mitch apologized, "Oh, sorry. I forgot about that. We could find a better place to sit."

Mike smiled. "Nah, I'm OK. What's up?"

Anderson casually leaned forward with his elbows on his knees, nodding toward Arnold Stadium. "I'll bet that sight brings back some memories for you. You did well for us on that field." He paused then looked directly at Mike. "Now that you are back, with your history and your new position here at WKU, I think you can help WKU football in another way."

He paused then looked directly at Mike. "What do you think about serving on the WKU Athletics Board? You'd be a great addition."

Mike was flattered by the offer, but his practical side made him hesitate. He pointed out that he had only seen college football from the bottom up and had little knowledge about what went on in such high places as the Athletics Board. "It does sound interesting, but I'm embarrassed to say that I really don't know much about it. I doubt that I have the expertise they need."

Anderson persisted, "Look, Mike, the Athletics Board is simply a university committee that considers various matters related to Western Kansas University sports and advises the university president and the academic senate. It has representatives from faculty, athletics, the student body, and some great nonvoting WKU supporters from town." He frowned. "My problem is that it is controlled by professors who, too often, see WKU football in a bad light. Sometimes I feel powerless to get what the football program really needs."

"And what's that?"

Anderson didn't hesitate. He banged his fist on his knee as he made each point, "More scholarships, more academic tutoring for athletes, more coaching staff! Yes, I know that some will ask, 'Why should football receive support that far exceeds that of many academic programs?' That question has an easy answer. Our team's success brings money to the university— money to support minor sports and the teaching programs in the Athletics Department. A realistic budget will convince our sponsors that the entire university is with our athletics programs—especially football."

Mitch looked down for a second then spread his hands and gave a shrug of his shoulders. "The situation is frustrating. I find myself asking, What the hell else can I do? You'd think that once I was on campus with the responsibilities I have and with the success our team has had, I'd have plenty of support from the Athletics Board. But that's not always the way it is.

"Many of the current board members don't really understand what football players have to put up with athletically, financially, or academically. Having you on the board—an experienced and successful WKU player, and now a prof, will go a long way towards keeping them informed."

Anderson stopped talking. He looked up and shook his head at his brief tirade. The sun had set, but its redness still illuminated some cirrus clouds feathering the evening sky.

"Sorry, Mike, but I have a problem with the university's over-control of the football program. We lost three players last year because of grades. Those guys just needed more help, not a boot off campus. There should be a better way to keep them.

"If we had someone on the board from the faculty—outside of athletics—someone who really understood WKU football, I believe a lot of these problems could be solved."

He looked directly at Mike. "I think you could be that person."

Mike paused to absorb Anderson's suggestion. He rubbed his forehead and glanced at Arnold Stadium in the distance. *Could he really do something useful on the board? Something for the football program?*

The coach persisted, "Mike, I know you. You understand, you've been on the field. You learn quickly. You can handle it."

Despite his time away from football field, Mike had no problem understanding Anderson's position with the current team. He smiled at the man who took him to the top of his game. "I can't say that I'm not interested, but academic positions on the Athletics Board are usually filled by full professors. I'm an untenured assistant professor. I doubt that either the president or the board chairman would go for it."

Mitch Anderson smiled and gave Mike pat on the shoulder. "You leave that to me."

After a few more words about the team and the whereabouts of some of Mike's former teammates, they parted with a promise to meet again over Mike's new opportunity.

8.

Mike and Laura's introduction over spilled food trays had led to further meetings in the cafeteria that were " just a tad calmer and quieter," as Laura laughingly described them. They easily slipped into conversations about their new teaching experiences and campus life in general. There was no doubt that they enjoyed each other's company, but both were still adjusting to new academic roles, and thoughts of anything akin to an actual date had been out of the question—until now.

Mike texted Laura's smartphone: *FBALL SAT? 2 GOOD SEATS*

She replied within minutes: *BUSY WI CLASS PREPS. SHUD SAY NO. BUT YES :)*

The following Saturday, they joined the noisy crowd pouring into Arnold Stadium. Both were dressed appropriately as Prairie Dog fans, especially Mike. Smiling and relaxed in tan board shorts, he wore a WKU red T-shirt with the white Prairie Dog logo. His curly hair was topped with a red baseball cap. Laura wore a sleeveless beige summer dress that—as Mike immediately noticed—showed off her trim, athletic figure. Her contribution to the WKU mania was a red broad-brimmed sunhat.

Mike led the way to box seats near the fifty-yard line, courtesy of Mitch Anderson. Laura looked around in surprise at their location. She spread her hands out to encompass the excellent view of the playing field. "Wow! I may not know a whole lot about football, but I do know prime seats when I see them. This is amazing, Michael." She reached over and gave a soft punch to his arm. "And I thought you were a new ' just paying off his loans' assistant professor."

Mike chuckled. "Well, as they say, it's who you know that counts. My WKU football alum status has gotten me a useful contact for tickets."

They leaned close to each other as the crowd noise increased. "I'm impressed, Michael, but I have to tell you, I'm going to take advantage of your football knowledge about those details of the game that have always escaped me."

Distracted by the sweet scent of her hair, Mike attempted to continue the conversation, "Aaa . . . errr . . . You don't understand American football?" "I spent more time in the swimming pool than at the stadium. Aside from tackles and touchdowns, I really don't know much."

He laughed. "C'mon, Laura! I'll bet those high school games taught you know more than you think."

Their conversation was interrupted as the opposing team jogged onto the field to distant cheers from the visitors' stands.

A flurry of trumpets and a rattle of drums announced the entrance of the WKU marching band led by a dozen cheerleaders. The home crowd was on its feet, shouting and clapping. The band was followed closely by the football team led by Coach Anderson and his assistants. They jogged onto the field with many players raising their helmets to the crowd. Fan noise decreased to a hum of talking and laughing as the teams spread out in the end zones to warm up with some stretches and a few plays.

Mike was in his element. He carefully checked players' positions, heights, and weights against lists in his program. He looked up at Laura. She seemed to be enjoying his pregame focus more than the action on the field.

He gave her an embarrassed smile and nodded toward the gridiron. "This is the first time I have been in this stadium in a while." He laughed. "I'm relearning the territory."

He asked, "Have you been to many games?" He kidded her with a gentle push on the shoulder. "You do know where the fifty-yard line is and what a down is, yes?"

She laughed. "Yes, Michael, I know what those are, but I'm certainly not a football expert. A lot of high school football games"—she laughed at the thought—"the dance afterwards was always more important! Did you play a lot?"

He nodded. "I did–four years in high school and then three seasons here at Western Kansas."

"Only three?"

He took a deep breath. "It was three. The last game of my junior year, I broke my leg." He smiled ironically, patting his right thigh. "That was it. No more football."

"What a disaster! I can't imagine your disappointment."

"Yeah, a lot of that, but there was a positive outcome. That injury changed my academic direction a hundred and eighty degrees. Thanks to my dad's encouragement and his science and math genes—he was an engineer—I went back to school, did a BS degree, then on to grad school. And now, after a lot of years"—he smiled—"I'm back at WKU!

He shook his head, clearing thoughts of tough times past. "Enough of that history—our Prairie Dogs are off and running!" Their quiet conversation was lost in the roar of the packed stadium at the kickoff.

Early in the first quarter, it was clear to Laura that Mike's focus was more than an ordinary spectator. He might not be wearing the uniform, but he was certainly in the game.

"C'mon, you guys! Can't you see that? They're overloading their defense to our right. Geez! The left side is wide open, go there! Ahh-ha, they got it—now there's a good fifteen-yard gain!"

At a time-out, Laura playfully bumped his shoulder with hers, pointing to the field. "Hey, Michael, are you here or out there?"

He looked over at her and shook his head with an embarrassed grin. "I suppose I am a little more focused on the action than your usual Saturday afternoon fan. I've been off this field for a long time. I have to admit, yeah, just for a second or two, I wish I was still out there, running, catching, blocking." He took a deep breath and nodded to Laura. "You're right. It's still part of me."

She put her hand on his shoulder. "I was kidding you, Michael. I think I understand. I suppose I do the same thing when I watch an occasional swim meet, although I'm not as passionate." She laughed. "I don't dream about it!"

Mike relaxed as the Prairie Dogs dominated the game with a couple of early scores. Laura took the opportunity to ask him about some details of the contest: formations, decisions to pass or run, substitutions. He kept one eye on the game while carefully and clearly explained them from a player's point of view.

He pointed out a halfback who was having a great game. Checking his program, Mike identified Ray Smith, a recent transfer student from a nearby JC. Mike didn't need to read any details about Smith's statistics.

He only had to watch him for a couple of quarters to be convinced that he was a special athlete.

The referee's whistle marked the end of the first half. The rumble of drums and blare of trumpets introduced WKU's marching band from the other end of the field. Mike and Laura stood with the crowd to enjoy the entertainment.

Mike's attention was interrupted by the thought of Laura's earlier comment—about him being passionate about football. Kind of a heavy term. Of course, he loved the game. He missed playing. Hmm. Maybe he was talking too much about himself. He turned his attention to Laura. "Tell me about your swimming."

Her eyes lit up. "I did mostly sprints and relays. I was serious in high school, and during my first two years in college, I swam in some run-up events to the Olympics. When I didn't make the cut, I figured I had better get a bit more serious about my studies. Probably a little like you, fortunately, without breaking my leg."

Their easy conversation contradicted the fact that they had only known each other for a short time. Mike glanced at Laura as she watched the halftime show. He saw a smart, pretty woman whose company was so enjoyable. He hadn't had such an experience in a long time.

Laura seemed to read his mind, saying, "This reminds me just how I've had my head buried in classes and research. This is a wonderful, relaxing break—the most fun I've had in ages! Michael, this is your game, your school, and your stadium. You have to teach me the ways of the Prairie Dogs!"

He smiled. "I've been out of my football helmet for almost ten years. That leaves lot of WKU football for me to relearn. Plays and players are different, some coaches are new, and the Dogs have a few different opponents." He sat up, shaking his head. "Sorry about my long explanation. It's probably best to think of both of us as new people on the block. We will learn together."

Mike and Laura were silent for a few seconds, musing over Mike's comment about learning together. *Together . . . hmmm.*

Laura took advantage of the lull in the crowd noise to raise questions on some other aspects of the game. "I can understand the reasons for most time-outs—injuries and yardage measurements and the like. But I've also noticed that sometimes a referee calls a time-out that doesn't seem to have a purpose. Everyone just stands around for a few minutes, then play resumes. What am I missing?"

"It's probably a commercial time-out. You wouldn't notice it if you were watching the game on TV. What usually happens is that the network is running a commercial that is a little long, so the game is purposely delayed until the commercial ends. Makes sense. The TV audience doesn't miss any play. I suppose that a TV time-out will occasionally give one team a slight advantage." He shrugged his shoulders. "On balance, it probably isn't a big deal."

Loud cheers from the fans and shouts from the teams and coaches on the field made conversation difficult, but Laura's curiosity was peaked. She raised her voice over the loud cheers from the stands and noisy shouts of coaches and players on the field with more questions.

"As close as we are to the field, I've noticed that the players' uniforms and helmets all have at least one logo for a commercial outfit. The team makes money from those ads, yes?"

"They sure do. Sponsorships of all kinds help buy top-of-the-line equipment. They help keep big-time university sports programs going. And there's no question, WKU football is certainly big-time."

Midway through the fourth quarter, Mike and Laura were on their feet with the raucous home crowd when the Prairie Dogs scored again, putting the game away. WKU spectators, led by the student section, erupted into a loud barking, howling sound that had Laura wrinkling her brow. "What on earth is that?"

Mike laughed and shouted over the noisy celebration, "The bark of several thousand Prairie Dogs. It's something you will hear at the end of every game!"

Laura haltingly attempted a Prairie Dog bark that sounded more like a bad cough that turned into an infectious laugh. "I think I need a little practice."

The crowd quieted for a few moments. Laura took advantage of the decrease in the clamor to tap into Mike's football experience. "Michael, I am really impressed with WKU's play. These guys must practice many hours. And you know, it makes me wonder how that affects a player's grades." She glanced back at the action on the field, shrugging her shoulders. "Maybe I'm just too new." She laughed. "Incomplete statistics! Back to the game!"

Suddenly, the WKU quarterback rolled to his right and fired a long pass for a touchdown. The stadium erupted in the loudest cheers of the game. Mike jumped to his feet, shouting over the crowd noise, "Wow! Laura, our Prairie Dogs are good! It's so great to be to be back in this old stadium! I am home!"

Laura smiled at Mike's antics. "I think you should be a poster boy for your team—out there with those cheerleaders!"

He laughed. "Despite my undergraduate behavior, you have to admit that this has been fun—a great game for two new profs!"

She agreed with a sparkle in her eyes, "Michael, the game was exciting, and watching you watch the game has been very entertaining!"

He winced. "Ah . . . am I really that bad? Sorry for my undergraduate behavior. Yeah, I know I'm a football fanatic of the first order, but the best part of this game has been being here with you!"

She gave him a soft punch on the arm. "You do go on, Mr. Football Guy." "And by the way, Laura, there's been another interesting development for your 'football guy.' It looks like I'm going to get even closer to the game. The head coach has nominated me for the WKU Athletics Board. Now I have another chance to get involved with the team"—he laughed—"but, this time, with no fear of injury!

"The board is made up of profs, coaches, students, and some outside supporters of WKU sports programs. It monitors policies and procedures for all university sports and makes recommendations to the president and the faculty senate when changes are appropriate. Football is the biggest sport on campus and the board's major focus."

She frowned at Mike. "I understand your interest, but a board appointment sounds like a lot of extra work for a new assistant professor. Do you really have the time?"

Clapping for his team as they lined up for their kickoff, Mike leaned toward Laura, raising his voice a notch. "I think I can handle it. The only problem may come from my department chairman. We'll see."

After a short return of the kickoff, the opposing quarterback hurried the first play as the clock ticked down. He dropped back and threw a long pass to an end sprinting down the sideline. The WKU safety easily picked off the looping ball, returning it nearly thirty yards.

"Five minutes to go, Laura. The Dogs have forced them into a panic mode. It's all over."

WKU spectators counted down the last few seconds on the clock to begin their raucous celebration. At the sound of the gun, Mike and Laura were on their feet with the rest of the crowd with more cheers and applause for the Prairie Dog players as they jogged happily off the field.

The sun was gone. The chilly early fall air caused departing WKU fans to turn up their collars or push their hands deep into their pockets. Laura and Mike finally separated from the crowd to walk toward her apartment. They both felt sort of an unstated wish to continue their date. "Laura, how about a beer?"

She paused for a few seconds, putting a finger on her cheek and wrinkling her brow. "Hmm . . . sounds good to me. Nah, I better not. I have to be the good prof tonight. I have a little—make that *a lot*—of prep work to do."

He nodded. "I think I know what you mean. My kitchen table—my desk—is piled so high with stuff to do that I'm eating my meals standing up. You're right, that beers better wait."

At Laura's door, they chatted for a few minutes. Mike glanced at his watch. He reached for her hand. "Laura, today was wonderful! How about another time? Lunch? Dinner?"

She laughed as she unlocked her door. "How about lunch? I'll buy! But I warn you, it'll be a cheap one."

Mike responded with a grin, "Wow! Free food! Just let me know when and where!"

They both felt an unstated wish to stay standing at her door. But then they touched hands for an instant, and he turned to walk to his apartment. After a few steps, he stopped and looked back at Laura, still standing at her door—to see her wonderful smile one more time and to hear her say, "Bye, Michael."

He strolled back to his apartment, with her soft voice echoing in his ear. *Everyone calls me Mike-except Laura. To her, I'm Michael—hmmm.*

9.

During Mike's walks across campus, he always made it a point to say hello to Tank Kozlowski when he saw him working at one of his many gardening jobs. But those encounters had only been short "hi's" and "Bye's." Then, one October night, Mike had a vivid dream about a long-ago game with his old football buddy. He awoke determined to visit Tank.

Three blocks north of campus, Mike stopped in front of the leaf-strewn steps of a home in a quiet residential section of Gardnerville. A sign on the lawn identified the place simply as Blossom Hill, a name he had gotten from Tank. Not quite knowing what to expect, he climbed the stairs, took a deep breath, and pushed the doorbell.

A few minutes later, one of the home's employees escorted Mike into the living room, where Tank's huge form overflowed an easy chair. The look on Tank's face told Mike that he wasn't quite sure who his visitor was. With a friendly smile, Mike walked over to him and put his hand on his friend's shoulder. "Tank, it's me, Mike. I promised I'd come see you. I finally made it."

At first, the conversation was one-sided, with Mike taking the lead. Tank gradually relaxed as the light of recognition finally flickered in his eyes. Mike encouraged him with a few questions, asking about Tank's friends here at Blossom Hill. Many of Tank's answers were simply nods and smiles or shrugs, but Tank was certainly communicating.

While they talked, a few fellow residents entered the living room; a couple of them said hi to Tank, while others seemed distant, hesitant at the sight of Mike—someone new in their space.

42

Twenty minutes later, a stout middle-aged woman in a white apron stepped out of the kitchen to announce that dinner would be served shortly. She invited Mike to stay. He begged off, explaining that he had more than enough work waiting for him back at his apartment. Tank seemed to grasp Mike's explanation and nodded. "Oh yeah, gotta work."

Mike and Tank walked slowly to the front door, chatting a bit about Tank's yard work at the university. They stepped up to the door just as it opened to admit a tall middle-aged gentleman wearing a light-brown suit and a tie. He carried a small black bag. Tank smiled and pointed to him, "That's Dr. Morgan."

Extending his hand, Mike introduced himself, "Hi, I'm a friend of Tank's, Mike Wolf."

"Hello, Mike, I'm Fred Morgan."

Suddenly more interested in dinner, Tank said a quick good-bye and headed into the dining room. Mike turned to Fred with a laugh. "It appears that when Tank is hungry, Tank is gone!"

They stepped back into the living room for a moment to chat. Mike explained that he was a new faculty member at WKU and an alum who used to play football with Tank. "Those are good memories. Tank kept a lot of our opponents off my back."

In his early fifties, Fred Morgan was a slender six feet tall with wavy red hair, a deep voice, and a relaxing manner. This was one of his weekly visits to monitor Kozlowski and a couple of his roommates. Fred explained that the Blossom Hill group home was a state-funded facility for men with mental disabilities caused by injuries of various sorts. He was one of several medical volunteers who supplemented the efforts of the relatively small university medical staff.

Mike was impressed. "Fred, if you have a moment, I have a couple of questions about Tank."

"Sure, I have time. Keep in mind that if some of your questions about Kozlowski get too personal, I'll have to skip those. I'll let you know if we get into that territory. Why don't we step outside for a few minutes? We will be out of earshot of the patients and can speak more candidly."

Mike and Fred Morgan sat on a bench on the front porch. The weather was pleasant. Mike took a deep breath of the fall air. "I'll try to be brief. I know that Tank had some type of brain injury in football, but he is an enigma to me. We were friends and teammates years ago, and of course we still are, but he is different now. There are moments when he seems nearly normal and able to connect, but most of the time, his thought processes seem to slow down. Today, there were a couple of times when I don't think he knew where he was or who I was."

Mike squirmed a bit in his seat, smiling apologetically. "I've studied a lot of science, but details about brain injuries are way outside my area of computer engineering. From the bit of reading I've done about football head injuries—there is so much of it in the news these days—I suspect that Tank suffers from CTE. Is that true?"

Morgan nodded. "Most likely, it is CTE—chronic traumatic encephalopathy. But we need to be careful here. A definitive diagnosis can't really be made until his brain can be examined"—Morgan shook his head apologetically—"after he dies."

Mike sat looking out a nearby window, thinking about Fred's words. He refocused on the psychologist. "I value my friendship with Tank. I wish I could help. To me—excuse my computer analogy—he seems to process information very slowly, if at all, and his storage area is either limited or difficult to access, sporadic at best. Any advice how I might help him? Will he get better?"

Fred responded thoughtfully, "Mike, your computer analogy is a good one. And your interest in Tank is welcomed. Too many of these people have no outside contacts at all.

"About your questions—as with many brain issues, the problem is complicated. You are correct, Tank's condition is likely due to one or more severe blows to his head. He is a bit higher functioning than some, but as you have observed, he shows some classic symptoms of concussion injuries including memory loss and an inability to make quick decisions."

Mike grimaced as he heard what he feared. "It's such a damned shame. We spent a lot of good times together back in those days—

playing football, chasing coeds, laughing at life. That personality has gone away. He's different."

"Variations from patient to patient are large. Fortunately, Tank seems to have avoided the anger and frustration card held by many victims of CTE. He gets on well with the others in this house. I suspect his huge size keeps a lot of problems at bay."

Gesturing toward the living room, Mike asked, "Does he watch football on TV?"

"Yes. For short periods. Probably the best development for Tank has been his work as a groundskeeper. He loves his job and occasionally brings home stories about his day with a rake or a shovel in his hand. In fact, he mentioned your name to me a couple of months ago."

Mike studied his hands for a moment as he absorbed this new information. He looked up at Fred. "Do you think my visits are helpful?" "That is a tough question to answer with a definite yes or no. Seeing the two of you interacting, I would say it is likely. He seems to enjoy your company. Just remember that when you speak with him, keep it simple in ideas and vocabulary. He will respond best to past experiences common to both of you—sometimes with a little reminding."

Fred checked his watch. "I'd better be on my way. Would you do me a favor, Mike? Here's my card. Drop into my office now and then and let me know how things are going with you and Tank."

After Morgan left, Mike went back inside the group home to say goodbye to the staff. He got a goodbye smile from Tank when he patted him on the shoulder at the lunch table.

Mike stepped outside and headed back to his apartment in the breezy autumn evening. There was a lot in his mind as he walked through the showers of leaves carried by each gust of wind. He shook his head at the thought of good old Tank. He used to be a happy, funny, smart guy. But now . . . damn football! He suddenly stopped, asking himself out loud, "What the hell are you saying, Wolf? Football is bad? C'mon. It's a rough game. Stuff happens!"

A few seconds later, he stopped again, with another infernal internal question: *Mike, why are you limping?*

10.

Near the end of November, a memo from the university president's office reached Mike's email box. It was, as Coach Anderson had promised, an invitation to join the Athletics Board beginning with the spring semester. Responding to his chairman's request to discuss the matter, Mike made his way down two floors to the Computer Engineering Department office.

The secretary glanced over the shoulder of a student standing in front of her desk. "Hi, Dr. Wolf. Go right in. Professor Johnson is expecting you."

Ed Johnson stood behind his desk, twirling the blades of the model of a modern windmill—a sophisticated aerogenerator. He pointed toward a chair. Mike sat down. "That is certainly a fine model, Ed. Do you have any like that in the field?"

Johnson acknowledged the interest with a fleeting smile. "Yes, we do, but we'll talk about that another time."

His smile was quickly replaced by a frown. "We are here to discuss your Athletics Board appointment."

He tapped an index finger repeatedly on the desk to emphasize his next words. "A seat on that board is a demanding task. You are a very busy new faculty member. Do you really have the time? As far as I know, there are no other assistant professors on the board roster. Sure, they are found on department-level committees but not at the university level. Why? It's obvious. There is some very important university-level business to be handled that requires experienced faculty." He paused. "I repeat, *experienced* faculty!"

"The hanging question is, Do you think you qualify?"

Mike was silent at first, wrestling with his chairman's challenge. He had thought about these things. Sitting on the edge of his chair, he replied evenly to his boss, "I agree that as a junior faculty member, this is just one more item in a long list of new commitments. Please believe me, I have given this invitation a lot of thought." He paused, looking directly at his Johnson.

"I'm sure I can handle it. You know that I've had a couple of class evaluations by students and senior faculty—all positive. You also know that much of the Athletics Board's time is spent on football, the largest and most successful sport that WKU engages in. I know about WKU football, especially from a player's perspective."

Ed stopped his pacing. Arms crossed, he looked down at Mike. "I appreciate what you say, Mike, and I certainly understand your interest and experience. But you must keep in mind that sports are a long way from your labs, lectures, advising tasks, and research commitments in this department."

He placed his hands on his desk and leaned forward to emphasize his next point. "You do know that if I disagree with your appointment to the Athletics Board, it will not fly."

Mike nodded. "Yes, I understand your—my—position."

The chairman put his hands in his pockets and looked up for a few seconds. He seemed to be studying the plaster on the ceiling. He looked back at Mike. "Given my uncertainty and your unique background, I offer you a compromise. You may accept the Athletics Board position with this caveat: if I become aware of any evidence that your board responsibilities are interfering with your duties as a faculty member in Computer Engineering, I will immediately order you to resign. Understood?"

"Understood."

11.

The break between semesters had been a welcome change in Mike Wolf's pressing schedule. It gave him time for a few sleep-ins and a couple of weekend afternoons to relax in front of the TV and take in the football playoffs around the country.

The Prairie Dogs had been defeated in the first playoff round to the frustration of WKU fans, especially Mike. It took a few days to get past his *coulda, woulda, shoulda* playoff analysis with head-shakes and a beer or two. He finally let it go with a *there's-always-next-season* attitude.

Semester break had also provided time for Mike and Laura to make a few visits to a coffee shop located a block from campus. They enjoyed those moments together, laughing at Laura's description of their brief meetings as exercises in *"Are you still alive?"*

A week before the semester break was over, Mike's TV was off, and he had returned to his kitchen table / desk to complete lecture and lab preparations for upcoming classes. Too soon, it seemed, spring semester with classes and advising was underway. Spring seemed to be a misnomer, given the snow still flying across the campus.

Assistant Professor Wolf realized that his experience teaching the previous fall certainly hadn't made him the best instructor around. Between his late-night, last-minute preparations, there was a lot of running—well, more like fast limping—from classroom to laboratory to the office and back again. He wasn't sure how much his students benefitted, but that first semester had been a real learning process for Mike, and he was convinced that in the spring semester, he'd be much better.

Yes, WKU was truly a "walking campus" with its many long paths crisscrossing the university grounds. Especially new WKU students often grumbled at the required hiking, as many of them called it. It was common to see them running between their dorms and their classes. Mike, on the other hand, found that it was good exercise—if he started early enough and he usually did. The weather didn't matter. On this late winter day, he wore a heavy jacket and a knit cap against the cool, blustery wind and the falling snow. He was headed for his office.

Jerry Larson looked up from his desk when his officemate opened the door and stood for a few seconds to brush the last flakes of snow from his jacket. It was the first time they had been in the office at the same time since semester break. Jerry exclaimed, "Ah ha, Professor Wolf returns to his lair! You look to be well rested and ready to dive into the follies of the spring semester."

"Hi, Jerry! Spring doesn't quite cut it yet. It's still Winter out there." He laid his briefcase on his desk as Jerry stood and walked over to a wall calendar displaying a warm tropical scene. Grinning, he said, "I love this calendar. It is so . . . so unreal, especially for us WKU Prairie Dogs."

Pointing to the third week in January, he gazed back at Mike with his best professorial look—hand on his chin, one eyebrow raised. "Tropics aside, my friend—here we go again. Those hungry students have flooded through the gates, looking for us and our words of wisdom! Are you ready?"

Mike sat down at his desk, shaking his head and chuckling at Jerry's antics. "I hope I am. I better be. Sure, I'm ready . . . I guess"

Jerry responded understandingly. "Hang in there, Mike. I've seen enough of your exchanges with students looking for help to know you are a good teacher—a natural. And your wind-power stuff looks like it is going well. Just keep pushing. And don't forget to enjoy yourself. We are lucky guys. We have a great job."

Jerry and Mike chatted for a while, recounting their semester break activities, both laughing at how quickly the break was over.

Mike finally excused himself. "Well, Jer, it looks like I am off to my next big adventure. I've been appointed to the Athletics Board—first meeting today."

Jerry raised his eyebrows. "Wow, Mike! That's big stuff. I thought you had to be tenured and have a higher rank for that kind of assignment. How did that happen?"

Mike recounted his experiences with WKU football in the past and Coach Anderson's recent invitation. "And I got Ed Johnson's OK. So here I go."

Jerry shook his head, smiling ironically. "Well, Dr. Wolf, all I can say is that you better be prepared to burn that old midnight oil. You're going to be a very busy guy."

That afternoon, Mike hustled across the snowy campus, excited to be back in touch with athletics—especially football. Athletics Board meetings were held in a conference room on the third floor of old Tower Hall. He was already curious about the tasks he would be assigned as a new member of the board.

In the distance, he caught sight of a groundskeeper clearing snow—a huge guy bundled up against the cold, working slowly but steadily, shoveling a sidewalk from side to side. He was made visible by the puffs of vapor that came out of his mouth. A few steps closer and Mike recognized Tank. He checked his watch. There wasn't enough time to detour to say hello, but Tank's appearance reminded Mike that he owed him another visit.

He bypassed Tower Hall's old and slow elevator and shuffled up the outside stairwell to the meeting room. He stepped into the warm environment where the Athletics Board members were engaged in several conversations around a long table.

More than just another conference room, it was a historical space in an equally historical building. When the university was founded over a hundred years ago, Tower Hall was its first permanent structure. The first classrooms and office were housed here. Important meetings that generated the future of Western Kansas University were conducted in this room. One wall displayed a few somewhat faded black-and-white photos of bearded professors dressed in heavy coats and ties, markers of the formality of the male-dominated environment of those early days.

As the university had expanded with newer buildings, this room became the focus of meetings devoted to athletics. Appropriately, other walls were filled with pictures celebrating memorable successes of WKU teams. Mike recognized a photo from his last football season championship season. He walked closer to see Tank's grinning face among the towering linemen. And yes, in the front of the group, there was Mike, number 46, sitting on his wheelchair. This room was a truly special place. He felt honored to be here.

Rory Kabat, the board chair and a senior professor in the Political Science Department, began the meeting with the introduction of Mike as the newest board member. Including non-voting representatives of the student body and the community, Mike counted eleven other members around the table. After a warm welcoming applause, Kabat turned to the business at hand. He summarized the issues the board would consider during the spring semester. Most were minor items—scheduling conflicts, NCAA rule changes, and a new hire in the Athletics Department. The meeting was brief and ran smoothly. After some general discussion and a few questions, it was adjourned.

An hour later, Mike was back in his office with class preparations. He was distracted from his work at hand by thoughts of the board meeting. His first encounter with that group had been enjoyable—especially with the nod Rory Kabat gave to Mike's football experience. Mike was confident that he knew the sport and understood its importance to the university. He was sure he could contribute.

12.

Assistant Professor Wolf sat in his office reviewing notes for an afternoon lab. His officemate, Jerry Larson, was absent for a couple of days to attend a conference, and Mike had happily taken advantage of the extra office space to boot up three computers to display some sequential lab material.

Mike moved purposefully between displays and keyboards, carefully tweaking code when he was interrupted by a knock on his open door. He looked up to see the familiar form of Ken Brady, one of Coach Anderson's assistants. Brady filled the doorway. A former professional football player, he was about six feet five and 270 pounds—still in great shape.

Brady wasn't on the coaching staff when Mike played. In fact, this was the first time they had met formally. Mike knew a little about the coach from his own observations at football games and from discussions with Mitch Anderson, the head coach. On the field, Brady worked mainly with defensive squads.

Now face-to-face, the assistant coach's size was magnified. Short hair topped his huge head that seemed to be connected directly to his thick, broad shoulders. Small and close-set eyes sat atop a nose that looked like a large acorn over a mouth stuck in a permanent scowl.

"Hi, Coach, come on in."

Mike stood to greet his visitor. His hand disappeared into his visitor's huge grip. The pleasantries stopped there. Brady immediately got to the point. His voice was deep, gruff, and loud. "I want to talk to you about one of our players."

Mike smiled to himself. *This was obviously a coach that players had no trouble seeing or hearing—or fearing! Perfect for the football field.* "Sure, have a seat. What's up?"

Despite his intimidating appearance, Brady was a little nervous as he deposited his girth on the chair in front of Mike's desk. His frowning glances around the room indicated that he was feeling a bit out of place with the stuffed bookshelves and computer equipment that filled the office. This wasn't his environment. Office time was low on his priority list. He spent a few hours a week in a shared space with five other Athletics Department part-timers— the football field and the gym were his venues Mike sat back down as Brady shifted uncomfortably on his chair. He leaned forward with his hands on the edge of Mike's desk. "The player's name is Ray Smith. He is a physical ed major."

Brady's voice seemed to bounce off the walls and metal cabinets. "I'm one of his coaches and, off the field, his academic advisor."

Mike replied, "I know who Smith is. I watched him last fall. He certainly had some great games—a hell of an athlete."

Brady agreed. "Coach Anderson has told me about your contributions when you were a hell of an athlete."

"Thanks, but was a long time ago."

"But I think it's fair to say that you're one of us."

Mike sat up on his chair and pushed some work aside. He leaned on his elbows and gave Brady a hint of a smile. "Fact is, Coach, I have been away from this place for so long that I'm really just reacquainting myself with Coach Anderson and getting to know his staff, you included."

Mike paused, expecting a response from Brady. There was none. "So, what do you want to tell me about Smith?"

Brady chose his words carefully, nervously rubbing his forehead with a huge hand and then rumbling on, "Smith has a problem. Ah . . . well, he has some . . . some academic challenges. I'm sure that, as a former football player, you understand. There are reasons. You know how it is—in the fall, practice, practice, then home games and travel to away games. Then there's spring practice.

"Most players can handle that schedule, but a few, like Ray, have problems."

He shifted his large body uneasily on the chair and leaned closer to Mike. "We've kept Ray eligible by registering him for some lower-division physical ed classes. After all, he's a PE major. But now he's a junior, and he's taken all his required classes that are . . . are manageable."

Brady leaned back on his chair, nervously rubbing his hands together. He seemed to be having difficulty finding the right words. He sat forward again, placing his hands back on the desk. "I'm wondering if you can help by taking Ray into your general ed class. You know, that broad, descriptive course for nonengineering majors. I think it's called An Early History of Engineering. He should be able to handle it. We are only a couple of weeks into the new semester, so late registration shouldn't be a problem."

Brady paused and looked down then looked intensely at Mike. "There is one more thing. It might be necessary to help him out. Give him some breaks so he can manage a passing mark and stay eligible." He growled, "We need him!"

It was Mike's turn to pause as he digested Brady's request. He took a deep breath and picked up a pencil from his desk.

"Coach Brady, Smith is certainly welcome in my class." He pointed the pencil at Brady. "But understand this. I'll require of him the same performance that I require of my other students— that includes successful completion of the required homework and passing of the scheduled tests. "And I'll be happy to address all study issues with Smith and help him prepare for quizzes and exams—as I would for any other student. In fact, if necessary, I can set up regular meetings with him outside of class and in addition to my regular office hours."

Brady interrupted, his voice a loud growl, "And give him that passing grade? Yes?"

Mike frowned. He looked directly at the coach. "To attain a passing grade, Smith must perform on tests and homework assignments at an acceptable level—the same level required of all other students. Yes, I'll be glad to work with him, but he must do the classwork and pass the exams himself."

Mike paused then said to Brady, "I want to be absolutely clear on this. Do *not* expect me to reduce his workload or give him a passing grade just because he is a star football player. Do we understand each other?"

The veins in Brady's bullneck bulged as he gripped the arms of his chair, staring furiously at Mike. "Look, we really need him!"

Mike stood and leaned forward with his hands on his desk to put his face a foot away from Brady's. He spoke quietly, "Coach, if Smith is willing to work on his class material, I'm willing to help him with his studies. But he must pass the course on his own. No exceptions."

Brady was silent for a few seconds. Then he stood, towering over Mike, raising his gravelly voice, "Thanks for nothing, Wolf. I think I made a mistake about who you are and what this university means to you as an alum, *especially* as a former football player!"

He turned abruptly, muttering as he walked out. "You son of a . . ."

13.

Saturday morning, Mike was at his kitchen table. He ignored the dishes stacked in the sink—stacked on last night's dinner dishes. He'd wash them later. There was a lab exercise to grade. Sitting back from his laptop, he was distracted by thoughts of his encounter with Coach Brady. He considered the fallout from that meeting one more time.

No doubt Brady was a jerk of the first order. On the other hand, there was Ray Smith. What were his priorities? It wasn't hard to conclude that, with Brady as his mentor, Smith's situation wasn't very good—another example of the gap that existed between football and academics for too many players.

Given his own past as a football player with a marginal academic record, Mike easily identified with Ray Smith. There wasn't a lot of help from the coaches back then either. But he was lucky in a strange sort of way. His broken leg tossed him off the field. It wasn't pleasant, but it was the beginning of a new life for Mike—a life beyond football.

He focused on his computer screen. Enough football, back to work . . . but not quite. A few minutes into a lab exercise preparation, he realized that his attempts to concentrate were useless. Football concerns kept returning, especially Smith's situation. He looked at his watch then back at his computer screen with a thought, *I need a time-out!* He laughed at his frequent use of that football term. Repetitive, but right on.

He suddenly realized that it was Saturday—almost Laura time! Whatever their schedules, a Saturday morning break had become a usual diversion for Laura and Mike. He grabbed his jacket and was out the door.

She stood waiting on the sidewalk in front of the cafeteria. She saw Mike a half block away, hands in his pockets, head down. She put her hand to her mouth to cover a smile. *This will be an interesting meeting. Professor Wolf is definitely in his cogitation mode.*

Laura stepped out into the sunlight to greet him. "I see by the frown on your face that you are mulling over an important issue, Professor Wolf." She gave him a warm smile, putting her hand on his arm. "Care to share any of . . . hmm . . . any of your mulling?"

Her touch relaxed Mike. He grinned at her. "Speaking of mulling, I do have an issue that I'd like to bounce off you. Let's grab some coffee and see if we can find a quiet table."

A few minutes later, they were sitting in a corner booth, well removed from the conversations across the room. Laura added a little milk to her cup and took a quick sip. "Ahh! I needed that. My last class yesterday was a bit argumentative. I think I am still reeling from a long exchange with a determined student." She laughed. "You know how those seniors can be. Fortunately, that is over, and here we are.

"So, Michael, just what is—as you put it—your issue? I'm curious."

Mike glanced down at his cup, organizing his thoughts. When he looked back at Laura, his smile was replaced by a wrinkled brow. "Do you remember seeing Ray Smith when we were at that first football game of last season? A halfback. He had a great game. In fact, he has had a super season. Truly one of the Prairie Dogs' stars."

Laura nodded. "I do remember you pointing him out to me. From what I saw, I'd certainly have to agree, he's a spectacular football player! Is there a problem?"

"He has some academic difficulties. His grades aren't very good, and if he doesn't get his act together by the end of the term, he'll flunk out."

Mike looked out of the window over Laura's shoulder. He grimaced. "I feel for Smith. I'd like to help. I'm just not sure how to do it and make a difference. Coach Brady, one of the assistants, has asked—make that *demanded*—that I take Smith into my general ed course and give him a passing grade no matter what.

"Of course, I refused. But I did tell Brady that I would be glad to have Smith take one of my general education classes. I told him that I would meet with him outside of class to work on the course material. But when I told him no passing grade for Smith unless he does his own homework and passes his exams, the coach gave me hell for not supporting the team. He stood up and walked out of my office."

Laura shook her head at the details.

Mike continued, "Laura, I really think Smith can be helped, but I'm not sure what I can do without Brady's cooperation. I suppose I could approach him again, but I'm convinced that that's a dead end when it comes to academic advising. Brady's just no help. No, I won't go there."

He shrugged his shoulders and shook his head. He was clearly frustrated. "What do you think? Maybe you can point me in a new direction. Any ideas?"

She looked at Mike over the edge of her coffee mug while taking a slow, thoughtful sip. Their relationship could still be described as platonic, but Laura was having a difficult time staying in that mode. Mike's concern for this football player seemed to her to be beyond anything she heard from any of her colleagues about a student in academic trouble. She found Mike to be almost passionate in his desire to help. An inner voice kept coming back to her, *Laura, this is a wonderful man!*

She put her cup down and reached across the table to touch his hand. "I have to say that your question is purely 'Michael Wolf.' You are the most caring, thoughtful guy I know."

Mike's face reddened at her comment. "A . . . I . . . c'mon, Laura, this is a tough problem. I really need your input."

She stifled a laugh at his embarrassment. "Sorry, Michael, I really meant it as a compliment."

He gave her a forgiving smile. "I guess I knew that, but you . . . me . . . sometimes I think we are in uncharted territory. Can we call a truce until the dust settles?"

It was Laura's turn to blush at Mike's reference to uncharted territory. She reached over and formally shook his hand. "That is a deal, Professor Wolf—a truce. Back to Ray Smith."

Laura looked down for a few seconds as she got her thoughts together. Finally, she said, "Michael, from your description of Brady, I agree, he is useless in this situation. Why don't you just bypass him and speak directly with the player. Yes, that's the approach—you talk to Ray Smith. He has the problem. Maybe the two of you can find a solution. Go directly to him." Mike sat back for a second, studying the thoughtful look in Laura's brown eyes, pondering her suggestion. "Laura, you know, that idea is so good and so obvious that I'm embarrassed to say that it never occurred to me." He tapped a finger on his forehead. "Thanks for shaking up my gray matter. I suppose that sometimes I get myself tied up in the university pecking order."

She smiled. "Anytime, Professor Wolf."

Mike glanced at his watch. "I had better get back to my apartment and my computer. It's jammed with work. Much to do. I suspect that you are probably facing a similar afternoon."

She nodded with a sigh as they stood to leave. They walked slowly to the cafeteria exit. With hesitant waves, each made their way back to their apartments.

14.

The next Monday, Mike formalized his decision to contact Ray Smith and invite him for a one-on-one meeting. As an Athletics Board member, he had access to players' contact information. He quickly emailed Ray, inviting him to his office to discuss his academic situation. As easy as the contact was and as much as Mike wanted to speak with this player, he knew that there was a good chance that his offer of help would be ignored.

It wasn't.

The following morning, Ray Smith's six feet two and 220 pounds of football talent appeared at Mike's open office door. Mike invited Ray in, reaching across his desk to shake his hand. "Hi, Ray, glad you could come. I have seen you carry the ball. Pretty impressive—congratulations on a great season!"

Ray smiled at the compliment. It was a blustery, cool day outside, and he was dressed in brown sweats with the hood of his sweatshirt hanging back over his shoulders. His short curly black hair was nearly hidden by a baseball cap that just covered the tops of his ears. A gold earring that looked like a tiny fist decorated the lobe of his right ear.

Mike's friendly demeanor seemed to relax him. "Thanks, Professor Wolf."

"Ray, you saw my email, so you know that the reason I asked you here is to try to help you with your academic problems. I know that several of your grades are creeping into the failure range. We need to do something about that.

"You probably know that Coach Brady asked me to help you out with your grade issues by taking you into my general ed class. Have you discussed our meeting with him?"

Ray shook his head. "No, I haven't, but another coach told me that Brady didn't have any kind words to say about you."

Mike frowned. "Yeah, Brady and I had a disagreement. His ideas of helping you out didn't quite match with mine. In my classes, students earn passing grades. I don't give them away. So, it won't be easy. But I can help increase the odds of passing if you decide to do some work."

Ray squirmed nervously on his chair, uncomfortable with the way the conversation was turning. "I don't get it. From what I heard about your meeting with Coach Brady, you weren't interested in helping."

Mike furrowed his brow as he considered his visitor's questioning face. "Ray, you have that wrong. I do want to help you. That's why I contacted you. Unfortunately, Coach Brady's idea of help is that a good grade should be a gift. My requirement is that it should be the result of your own efforts." Mike clasped his hands and leaned forward. "There's a difference. I asked to see you because I'm willing to show you how to do the work to pass the course. Clearly, you are a smart guy. What you must do to solve this academic problem is apply the discipline that makes you an outstanding football player..

"Ray, I don't want to kid you. You are in trouble academically. If you want to stay around to play more football, you must put your head in the books. I am offering to help you get your studies together."

Ray blinked, raising his eyebrows. "You will help . . . me?"
"Definitely. But it's a two-way street. You must do the work—whatever it takes."

Ray showed hesitant interest in Mike's offer. He nervously rubbed his hands together. "What would it take?"

"Let's start out with some facts. You are listed on the roster as a junior. Can you tell me what classes you are taking, and what grades you expect in those courses by the end of this semester?"

Smith leaned back, closing his intense brown eyes for a few seconds. Mike's office was suddenly very quiet as his visitor put his hands to his face. When he looked back at Mike, his words painted a grim picture. "I haven't really thought about it that much. Finals are still a few months away."

He paused, looking away from Mike as he mentally reviewed his academic status. He finally answered, "Hmmm, what grades? Let's see, English 20: D, PE 205: A, History 3: D, Geography 57: D, Math 12: F." Before Mike could ask the next question, Smith gave him the answer:

"I know, those grades give me a grade point average well below C. It isn't the first time. You probably already know that I'm on probation this semester."

Mike sat back. "Ray, you've got to make some changes, or you will be out of here."

Ray's lips were tight as he nodded at Mike's comment.

Mike rubbed his forehead, finding it difficult to be positive about the situation. He finally took a deep breath, saying, "Look, Ray, we have some time left in the spring semester, and I'll help as much as possible."

"To be honest, Professor Wolf, I know my situation looks pretty bad. Yeah, I might be able to pull up the grade in my geography class. But without a miracle, my other grades will knock my grade point average down." Shaking his head at his situation, he said, "On top of that, spring practice is coming up. If this spring is like last year, I'll be too busy to study a whole lot."

Mike was quiet for a few seconds, reviewing his notes on Ray's grade estimates. He looked back at his visitor. "Ray, consider another possibility: we can set up a formal, regular tutoring session, say once a week—more if you need it. Just you and me. We can work together to try to fix this.

"I want you to understand that I wouldn't make this offer to just anyone. I only do it here because I think you are smart enough to do the work in your classes—it's just that football has gotten in the way." Mike sat back, crossing his arms, looking directly at Smith. "I know that problem—I've been there."

"I'll tutor you, but you must agree to do some extra work. And you must remember that I can't take your exams for you or just hand you the grade you want. In the end, a positive result is up to you."

Smith sat quietly for a moment, looking down at a silver cup full of pens and pencils on the front of Mike's desk. A sad look in his intense brown eyes told Mike that, until this moment, he hadn't really given much thought to how poor his chances were to be back in the fall. For the first time, he was facing the fact that he might not be around for the next season. His voice was almost inaudible as he mumbled, "Thank you for your offer, Professor Wolf, but it's too late. I think I have been kidding myself."

Ray gave the distinct impression that the meeting was over as he pushed his chair back from the desk. He gave Mike a look of resignation. "I know you were a pretty good football player a while back, Professor Wolf, so you know that there is hardly enough time to be a student and a good football player. You are smart, you made it. I'm not so smart."

"Ray, my path to where I am today had a few bumps. When I played football, I wasn't such a great student either. Sure, I was a pretty good football player, but in the end, that didn't matter. I got hurt—no more football.

"When I realized that football wasn't going to be part of my life, I left college. My own lousy grades weren't doing me any good, so I walked away from WKU. Failing was my own doing. Getting hurt only rubbed my nose in it.

"I finally came back to the university to find something after football. It took a long, long time. If I had had some different advising and some academic encouragement when I played football, my road to finishing my degree would have been different. A little smoother—definitely shorter." Ray's arms were crossed. His eyes no longer connected with Mike. His headshakes told Mike that he was frustrated with the situation—including

Mike's so-called solution.

Mike spoke quietly, almost pleading, "Look, Ray, you aren't hurt, but your poor grades will be the end of college for you. You have to do something different if you want to stay around. I can help."

Ray looked down, embarrassed as tears appeared in the corners of his eyes. He covered his face with his hands as he came to grips with his situation.

"Ray, think of it this way. Your academic problem is like trying to be a great football player. You must do the work—put in the time, take a few hits, persist—to get the results you want. I can't guarantee that you will be here next fall. But if you take my offer of help, you will learn a few things and you just might stay in school.

"I think it's worth a try. I'll help. It's up to you. Do you want to do it?"

Ray was frustrated, suddenly raising his voice, "I just want to play football! That's all I want to do. College courses get in the way!"

He was devastated at the likelihood of a premature end to his collegiate football experience. Mike knew that their discussion had touched on realities that Ray had been purposely ignoring—all that stuff he just didn't want to think about, such as *what's next?*

He looked at Mike. "Professor Wolf, I don't have enough experience for the pros. A couple of scouts have contacted me, congratulating me on a good game or two, but that's all. They know and I know that I need to get bigger and have more experience in college ball. I'm just not ready."

Head down, elbows on his knees, he whispered, "If I just had another year."

Ray got up slowly and stood behind his chair with his hands in his pockets. With a shrug of his shoulders, he slowly turned for the door, absently inspecting one of Mike's old team photos on the wall of the office. "Maybe I could try out for a pro team in Canada or maybe even a semipro team—somewhere."

His words became a whisper, "I really don't know what to do."

"Ray, I invited you here to offer some help. That offer still stands."

Smith stopped for a moment with his hand on the doorknob. In a resigned whisper, he said, "It's too late, Professor Wolf."

He pulled his cap on and quietly left the office. Mike's words chased him down the hallway, "Don't give up on it, Ray. My door is open."

15.

The arrival of spring brought some pleasant days to the WKU campus. Assistant Professor Wolf was in a good mood. Lectures were in shape, and labs were running well with some new hardware and software modifications that he had developed over semester break. All required constant efforts in his office and at home, tweaking class presentations and online material and keeping up with grading.

Mike also made some definite progress in his research. Big help were the efforts of his two graduate assistants who had come up to speed on projects late last semester. Yes, things were moving along.

There were also some interesting developments outside of work. Saturday evenings often found Mike and Laura walking a few blocks from campus to have a pizza and a beer. Mike had been determined to keep the " just friends" part of their relationship valid. A good idea, but lately, he was finding thoughts about Laura slipping into his consciousness at unexpected times. Just yesterday, in one of his lecture classes, one of his female students leaned over to whisper something to a fellow sitting next to her just as Mike looked up from his computer. Her slim figure and short hair interrupted his concentration with a mental picture of Laura. He hoped no one noticed the hiccup in his presentation as he shook that image out of his head and refocused on his lecture material.

The brighter spring sun also found Mike becoming more comfortable with his Athletics Board involvement. Chair Rory

Kabat had recently asked him to compare some board practices at WKU with those at other universities. The assignment worked particularly well with Mike's desire to brush up on current rules and policies governing football. There had been a few minor changes since he played. Useful information.

On the afternoon of the last Friday of March, he hurried across campus to a board meeting. He scanned the sky with the eye of a true Kansan as he walked. *Uh-oh, some growing cumulus clouds with a few anvils to the southwest.* He thought, *Yep, I'm back home, and here come the thunderstorms!* With a little luck, the rain would hold off until he got back to his apartment after the meeting. He shook his head with a smile. *Probably not.* Crowds of WKU students filled the well-used sidewalks between campus buildings. Clearly in their heading-for-the-weekend mood, chatter and loud laughter accompanied each group he passed. In another few hours, many of them would return to jam the campus arena for an evening basketball game.

Tower Hall presented its usual challenge for Mike to get to the conference room. Steps—lots of steps. Fortunately, he was early. He could climb slowly while he turned his mind to the tasks at hand. He had been reading incessantly to learn more about the WKU Athletics Board and its responsibilities. Blessed with a quick mind and his love of sports in general, he absorbed the information quickly. Even with his teaching and research commitments, he felt that this new assignment suited him well.

Those already at the conference table nodded and smiled at Mike as he took his seat. It was clear that the effect of the warmer spring weather had also washed over them.

Rory Kabat tapped his gavel twice, bringing silence to the table. The relaxed mood of the board members was dampened quickly as he made an ominous announcement. "Allegations of a serious cheating incident involving several of our current football players have come to my attention." Kabat cleared his throat as surprised and concerned looks were exchanged around the table. He consulted his notes then looked up at the group.

"I don't have complete details yet. However, the preliminary evidence indicates that this problem goes beyond a single random infraction. It appears to be a well-organized effort by a significant number of players in collusion with some students outside of the football squad."

He reached for the glass of water and sipped slowly. Then, clearing his throat, he went on. "We all know that occasional cheating on exams by a few athletes is not new.

"When those instances are discovered, they are usually dealt with by the instructors, and the results are reflected in individual grades of the guilty player. What is unusual in this latest case is the number of players involved and the apparent organization to steal test information and alter grade records."

Kabat walked slowly around the conference table with his arms crossed, looking from face to face. As he reached the opposite end of the table, he paused, placing his hands on his hips. His military bearing was apparent. He raised his voice a notch, "This is trouble, people! If just half of these allegations are true, we have a major problem on our hands."

He returned to his seat and looked up at the unusually quiet group. "Comments?"

Tim Barnes, the director of WKU Athletics, raised his hand to be recognized by Kabat. Known as one of the most successful athletics directors in the Midwest, at fifty years old, Barnes looked the part of an athlete. His six-foot-five height and lithe build reflected his success as a former All-American basketball player. After earning degrees in physical education and business at the University of Wisconsin, he coached college basketball at a small college for a short time. But he had bigger plans. Over the course of about ten years, he redirected his efforts to the application of good business principles to collegiate sports in general.

Barnes arrived at WKU with experience and success in rebuilding athletics programs at two smaller institutions. He believed strongly that the university benefited greatly from successful athletic endeavors. Occasional criticisms by some academics for his tough business attitude regarding all sports on campus were more than balanced out by extensive praise he received for the many accomplishments of the WKU teams, especially football.

His self-assured manner was evident as he sat forward to address the board members, his hands placed widely on the conference table. He looked from face to face and spoke clearly and confidently, "You can be sure that any kind of cheating, on or off the field, does not resonate with my ideals of athletic competition.

"Although I haven't seen all the details of the current investigation, it is my impression that this is one of those situations where a few ball players did something pretty stupid.

"I certainly don't defend such behavior. As Professor Kabat has pointed out, infractions by a few players have happened before. We must certainly discipline those responsible and minimize those occurrences in the future. At the same time, let's not allow ourselves to fall for the old 'bad apple' argument. We shouldn't let the fallout from the actions of a few land heavily on the many honest players in our fine football program." Barnes waved his hands in a dismissive gesture. "Trust me, this so-called investigation will not find much. In the meantime, I ask everyone to keep this minor problem in perspective and concentrate on our football successes."

The next board member to speak was Ralph Bennett. He represented the Chamber of Commerce of the city of Gardnerville. Bennett was in his sixties. His back was bent somewhat—the result of an auto accident a few years ago. That posture and a scratchy smoker's voice belied his fine athletic past. His relation to WKU and to football was rooted in the four years he spent as a linebacker for the Prairie Dogs. Brash and outspoken, there was no doubt about his staunch support of the WKU football program.

Bennett scoffed at the alleged infractions. "These so-called accusations are ridiculous. We are here to enhance our fine football team, not to condemn it. There must be more important items on our agenda."

Mike, in his short time on the board, had heard many other comments from Bennett dismissing negative opinions of the football program. This time he had the support of scattered applause from like-thinking members of the board. One of those was from John Roach, another representative of the off-campus community.

Roach, now in his late fifties, was a long-time resident of Gardnerville. An automobile and truck dealer, he was well-connected to the city and the surrounding agribusinesses. As a young man, his attendance at WKU was highlighted by three seasons as an excellent Prairie Dogs' football player. Unfortunately, his academic performance was not on par with his football efforts, and he decided to drop out of school before he flunked out. The end of his college days saw him take a part-time job selling cars. He was an excellent salesman and developed into a successful manager. Over the years, he established his own highly profitable auto sales business, donating substantial amounts of money to WKU sports programs.

Now, in middle age, Roach was bald, fat, and red-faced, despite his past as a superb football player. His long-established salesman personality dominated interactions with Rory Kabat and the rest of the members. In any discussion about WKU sports, his strong support for the university and its sports, especially football, came through loud and clear.

He adamantly denied the seriousness of the alleged cheating incident, pounding his fist on the conference table. "Ralph Bennett is absolutely right! We must keep in mind that college football at this institution has been a boon to this university and to our local businesses. Let's keep these incidents in perspective!"

Bennett and Roach served on the board at the invitation of the president and the recommendation of the mayor of Gardnerville. Nonacademics on various WKU boards weren't unusual. Although they were nonvoting members, they were important in the development of various academic programs and in maintaining good university-city relations.

Mike originally assumed that that such representatives on the Athletics Board simply acted as a conduit of information between university sports and the city, for example, to minimize problems that might arise from competing city / university events. The loud opinions of Bennett and Roach cast doubts on that assumption. They spoke as if they were voting members.

Mike, somewhat amazed by the rhetoric of the townspeople, maintained a low profile in the discussions. His mind-set regarding his role as a new board member was that he would learn more by listening. This discussion was a perfect example.

When the loud retorts by Bennett and Roach about the alleged cheating incident ended, the conference room becoming unusually quiet. Kabat glanced around the table—there was no further discussion. He gaveled the meeting to an end with the decision to wait for more complete information before taking any action. The participants slowly rose from their chairs and departed the conference room without the usual friendly chatter that followed most board meetings.

16.

Leaving Tower Hall, Mike's previous expectations of a thundershower proved correct. He hurried to his office across campus, just managing to reach the steps of the engineering building as the heaviest rain began to fall.

A few minutes later, he sat at his desk, booting up his laptop. Mike's home page was not the usual picture of familiar faces or a beautiful outdoor scene. The opening screen displayed his updated to-do list. He had gotten into the habit of posting daily reminders on his home page as a grad student—the routine stuck. His officemate kidded him about it. "Mike, you need a relaxing picture to start the day—a Kansas wildflower or a sunset." He laughed. "Maybe even a picture of your girlfriend!"

Mike smiled and shook his head. "Sorry, Jerry, no girls. My checklist is a great way to get me moving for the day. You should try it."

Jerry waved his smartphone in the air. "This is my way! I carry it in my pocket and enjoy a picture of my kid's grin to start my day."

"I'm not quite to the 'my kid' stage yet," Mike replied. "Maybe in a few years, if I ever have time to find someone who would care for a limping ex-football player."

Mike and Jerry chatted for a few more minutes then turned back to the work at hand. Mike's important to-do items included a lecture to review, an update for his afternoon lab, an appointment with a graduate student to deal with some problems with her thesis project, and an abstract to submit for a presentation at an upcoming engineering conference in Kansas City. He took a deep breath as he looked at his list. One of his rules was to keep it on a single page. He recalled that, in graduate school, sometimes the only way to do that was to make the font smaller. He laughed at the thought. *Well, I may be busy again, but at least I'm still in normal font size!*

His officemate looked up from his computer with a wrinkled brow. "Wolf, what in the hell are you muttering about?"

Mike swiveled his chair around to face Jerry. "Sorry for the interruption, Jer. Nothing to worry about, I'm just in a major organizing state."

Jerry shook his head with a smile. "Oh, these new assistant professors and their occasional weirdness. Hopefully it will pass."

Mike agreed with another chuckle. "Me too. I can't wait to be normal!"

Mike turned back to inspect his to-do list. Jerry's joking suggestion about putting a picture of his "girlfriend" on his computer screen immediately brought Laura to mind. This interruption was not a new experience. Over the weeks and months since they met, he felt that Laura certainly counted Mike as a close friend. Anything beyond that was lost in her class preparations and oceanographic work . . . *but then* . . .

Mike found himself thinking about Laura's wonderful personality, her brains, and her beauty. He told himself that he was lucky to have her just as a good friend. He tried hard not to consider anything else . . . *but then* . . .

These mind-sets resulted in particularly interesting behavior. For example, the word *date* was still not used in their conversations. "Meet for coffee?" was probably their most common excuse for calling each other. Those twenty-minute get-togethers in a quiet corner of the cafeteria were typically squeezed into their busy schedules a couple of times a week. Conversations were light. But if anyone watched their body language, it was clear that there was something special between them—whether they knew it or not.

* * *

On a Friday afternoon, Mike sat at his desk across from one of his graduate students, Sam Schwartz. They were discussing a coding problem related to Sam's thesis when Mike's phone rang. It was Rory Kabat.

"Mike, we need to talk. It's important. More evidence has been uncovered about the cheating problem we discussed in our last meeting. The allegations are grim. I want to brief you on what we know to date. There is work to do."

"Can you give me a half hour? I'm meeting with a student right now." "That's fine. I'll see you then."

Mike turned back to Sam for another twenty minutes, finally reaching a workable solution to the coding problem. "Thanks, Professor Wolf, this was easier than I thought. I guess I just needed a couple of hints."

"Your approach was correct, Sam. You just needed to push it through to the end. Hang in there, keep working for efficiency, especially when you want to loop solutions. It will get easier. Remember my two basic rules for figuring this stuff out."

Sam stood to leave, zipping up his computer bag. He laughed. "Yeah, I know, I know—practice and persist!"

Mike grabbed his briefcase and hustled over in the office of the chairman of the Athletics Board. He barely sat down when he listened to Rory read a three-page document he had just prepared. It detailed the latest information about the cheating incident investigation. When he finished, he looked up and shook his head. "I've been around college sports for a long time, Mike, and I have never seen anything like this. Now we've got to put our heads together to develop a response.

"The final document will come from the president's office, but she will lean heavily on the board for advice. Take this draft with you—it is not for public release yet—and come back with your comments by . . . by tomorrow? Can you do that?"

Mike nodded. "Can I email them to you?"

Kabat shook his head. "No email. Hand-carry your response to my office. You will see when you read the report that there were some computer techs involved in this. Most likely our email is safe, but I don't want to take any chance for a premature release of our discussions."

Mike scanned the report on his way back to his office, stopping occasionally to read some sections in detail. If half of the charges were true, the team, the board—the whole university—had a lot to think about. The word *cheating* had taken on a deeper meaning

During his own playing days, he had been aware of teammates who had cheated on exams and other academic projects. At the time, his impression was that a few players who were too tired or too lazy to study had done some stupid things such as carrying cheat sheets into examinations. His own grades weren't so great back then, but he didn't cheat. In fact, he noticed that the few teammates who did so rarely gained anything in the long run.

Athletes who were marginal students often played out their eligibility but never completed a degree. Faces of some of his teammates appeared in his mind's eye. Lewis didn't graduate; Sterner didn't graduate; Connors flunked out. Even Mike, with his broken leg, had dropped out just before he flunked out.

The present cheating situation was different. The organization went far beyond looking over another student's shoulder to copy an answer or carrying a page of answers into an exam—not that those efforts were right. They just seemed to be innocuous compared to the current organized scheme.

Jerry Larson looked up from his computer screen as Mike walked into their office. "Hey, roomie! Those furrows on your academic brow tell me that you need a break."

Mike smiled at Jerry's comment as he tossed his briefcase on his desk and glanced at his watch. "Hi, Jerry. You know, I think you're right. My next class isn't for a couple of hours. I hear the cafeteria and a cuppa calling my name. Why don't you walk over there with me and I'll buy you one? Got time?"

Jerry shook his head. "Thanks, but I have a student coming in in about ten minutes with—so he says—an unsolvable lab problem." He shook his head with a knowing smile. "I'd better hang around."

Mike stood at his desk. "Well, I'll tell you what, Jer, how about I drink a second cup for you?"

Jerry laughed. "Get out of here, Professor Wolf. Go drink your coffee."

17.

Despite the gloomy report on the football problem, Mike enjoyed his walk toward the cafeteria. His limp was barely noticeable. A warm spring breeze ruffled the light-green foliage along the path. Laura was on his mind. He stopped at the edge of the sidewalk and pulled out his iPhone to call her.

She answered immediately. "Hi, Michael! I was just thinking about you. What's up? How is the engineering-football guy doing?" She laughed. "Busy as ever, I bet."

"Well . . . I suppose I'm a little busy, but not so busy that I'd skip sharing a donut and a coffee with you. In fact, Laura, I'm just now walking over to the cafeteria. Interested?"

"Good timing, Michael. I have just finished putting together an exam for my general biology class, and I could really use a breather too. Let's see . . . I've got an hour or so. Let's do it!"

Ten minutes later, Mike carried a tray with their cups and a to-be- shared slice of cake to a table near a bright window in the cafeteria. He sat down with an audible sigh, "Whew, do I need this!"

Laura cut the dessert in half and pushed the plate to the center of the table. "Here is some sustenance, Michael. Sounds like you could use it."

He nodded with a weary smile. "You're right. I don't see how you do what you do and look so calm and collected anytime I see you. Sometimes, I think I'm going crazy with my own class preps, grading, committee stuff, etc., etc. I eat most of my meals—if you want to call them that— standing up."

He reached across the table and touched her hand. "And it seems like I haven't seen you in weeks."

"Why, Michael, that is a very nice compliment. Thank you! I've missed our meetings too!"

Mike's face glanced at neighboring tables, wondering if anybody noticed these two faculty members holding hands—sort of. He reached for his cup with a stammer. "Aaa . . . well . . . like I said, I've been busy. That's it—busy."

Mike shook his head and refocused. "Laura, a screwy problem has come to my attention. Something related to my Athletics Board work. It's a bit complicated. I wondered if you'd mind if I shared some of the details with you. I need an independent opinion."

She nodded, sensing the seriousness of the situation. Mike ran his hand through his hair as he organized his thoughts. He looked up at Laura. "In a nutshell, this is the deal. One of the assistant football coaches is pressuring me to take a failing football player into one of my lower-division classes and give him a passing grade, no questions asked."

Mike described his meeting with Brady over Smith's academic situation.

"Michael, it sounds to me that you handled Brady OK. Otherwise, it seems to be a problem without an easy solution. He's a jerk, and you don't rattle easily. Sounds like an infinite confrontation if you continue to do business with him.

"But I see a larger issue here. You are giving a lot of your energy to your new board assignment. As one new busy assistant professor to another, do you really have the time?"

She watched Mike closely as he glanced out a nearby window, absorbing her comment. Yes, she was concerned for this thoughtful, dedicated fellow who invested himself thoroughly in his work. "Michael, maybe you are a bit overcommitted."

He smiled at her. "Laura, thanks for your interest. Obviously, I don't think that I am overcommitted. It's just that life has always seemed to come at me in bursts. Sometimes I am insanely busy, other times, I can kick back and have a beer." He shook his head with a resigned smile. "My current situation certainly qualifies as one of those insanely busy times—for good reason."

Laura frowned. "Michael, I understand your desire to help, but you are a junior faculty member and brand-new on the board. Are they going to listen to you?"

He was quick to answer. "Somebody is listening, or I wouldn't have been given this assignment. Especially if there are some problems with WKU football—*the* major sport on campus. I can help."

The doubtful look on Laura's face told Mike that he hadn't quite convinced her. He tried again. "Why me? I'm in a unique position. I received my undergraduate degree from WKU, I'm ex-WKU football player, and I'm a WKU faculty member. There is no other board member who has that background. Yes, I'm busy, but I think I can handle the appointment to the board, and I know I can contribute."

Laura crossed her arms and looked at Mike. "Michael, I have no doubt that your unique background is something the board can use." She shook her head. "But I must be honest with you—it sounds like it's too much."

He paused and glanced out a nearby window as he put his thoughts in order. Then he looked back at Laura. "You're right, I do have some other responsibilities. But—pardon the football analogy—I've taken the ball, and now I've got to run with it. No looking back."

She looked at him over her cup and said, "I'm only just beginning to understand you, Michael Wolf. Your honesty and dedication are something to behold! It's just that there is a thin line between *enough* and *too much*, and you seem to be straddling it.

"Just be careful. I wouldn't want you to hurt yourself, either physically or professionally."

Mike put his cup down and took a few seconds to look into her beautiful eyes. "Thanks, Laura. Believe me, I take your comments seriously. Your support is very important. Not to worry, I can handle this. It'll work out." He reached across the table to touch her hand. "We've been talking too much about' *my* problem. Tell me how things are going with your classes and your research."

"Michael, I appreciate your interest, but it's you that I'm worried about. Please think about this: you're in danger of being overwhelmed by the combination of your teaching and research responsibilities and this board assignment."

Mike put his hands over his face. She could see his smile between his fingers. He put his hands down on hers. "Professor Sparks, you generate a warm and fuzzy feeling in the brain of this guy. I don't think either one of us can define it—suffice to say, it's good—very good."

She blushed and gave him an embarrassed smile.

"I'm OK, Laura. I can handle this. Please . . . do not worry."

She took a deep breath. "OK, Mr. Football Guy, since I can't convince you to reconsider your board assignment, maybe it would help if you told me about what you call *the football problem*—if you want to. We can talk about my work later."

Mike looked down at his cup then nodded, saying, "Thanks, that would help. Let's take a walk. It would be better to be out of earshot of our neighbors at the next table."

Laura looked up at Mike as they strolled across a quiet part of the campus near the creek. "So, Michael, just what are you keeping bottled up?"

They found a bench to sit on. No one was in sight.

Elbows on his knees, chin in his hands, Mike looked down for a second. Then, he rubbed his forehead and sat up. "Here's the short version. There has been evidence of a serious cheating incident here at WKU. It involves several many WKU football players."

Mike looked across the creek and shook his head. "When I was on the team, I was aware of occasional cheating by a few of my teammates— stolen exams, essays bought and sold for money, cheat sheets. I didn't do it. Cheating was their choice. They were football players. They did what they felt what they needed to do to stay on the team. Of course, being on the team for four years still didn't mean that they graduated. You know that I had my own academic problems when I was a football player."

He was agitated—clasping his hands together, looking down, and shaking his head. "My attitude was always 'That's life!' You had to pay the price for your own bad behavior. It's what happened when good football players had marginal academic qualifications.

"Today, a light seems to have gone on in my head. I finally understand that it isn't just the individual players, it's the system—the business of football—that drove them to cheat in my day and drives them to cheat today.

"Between practice and games, especially games that require travel, the time available for a typical player to attend classes, do homework, and study is greatly reduced. Online components of classes can help, but then there is always the tiredness factor."

Laura was fascinated as she watched her companion, the cheering Football Mike, transform into a somber Professor Wolf as he analyzed the academic dilemmas of players. He was serious and concerned—and he was torn. She realized that he was finally saying something that had been on his mind for a long time. His Athletics Board appointment wasn't just an interesting and exciting way to reconnect to his athletic days. It was a wake-up call.

Mike gazed at the nearby creek, as if he was searching for an answer in the water bubbling over the rocks.

"So what's the result?" He laughed at his own question. "I could be a sort of a poster boy for the process. I didn't cheat, but my grades were terrible. If I hadn't dropped out of college after my injury, I would have flunked out. All because of my focus on football. WKU football."

Laura tried to lighten Mike's mood. "Michael, don't be too hard on yourself." She pointed to Arnold Stadium visible in the distance. "I would bet that the football fanatics who fill that place every game would agree with you—American football has its problems. It's nothing new."

He nodded. "You're right, Laura, cheating among football players isn't a new problem. It's just that the current situation with our Prairie Dogs is beyond anything I have ever experienced."

He gave an ironic half smile. "In some ways, my football days are coming back to haunt me. This infernal cheating problem has been the trigger. I suspect that you will hear details soon enough—when the investigation is made public. For now, they are the headache of the Athletics Board." He laughed. "And I'm now one of those sage members who must find a solution."

He stood up, turning to look at Laura. "I have kept you too long, Professor Sparks. We both have work to do."

She patted him on the shoulder. "Thanks for trusting me with the details of the board situation. I agree, it's a tough one. And I do understand why you are so involved, despite all your other responsibilities. You'll handle it, Michael, but please get some sleep. You are going to need it!"

"Thanks, Laura, this discussion has helped calm me down. Not to worry, Dr. Sparks, I'll be OK." He smiled. "Your voice is like sweet music to my ears!"

"Why, Michael, that is almost romantic!"

He was silent for a few seconds. "Well, I . . . er . . . umm," he stammered. "I didn't mean . . . now don't get me wrong." He put a hand up to his reddening face, with a muffled "Oh, geez!"

Laura's laughter was infectious. She pointed at the cluster of university buildings in the distance. "We better get back to work, Dr. Wolf. I think that place needs us!"

They strolled toward their offices, both aware of the moment when their hands accidentally touched. Mike wasn't sure what the effect on Laura was, but for a moment, a bolt of lightning from one of those prairie thunderstorms found its way to his hand.

Saturday evening found Mike in his apartment. A little after 9:00 p.m., he had just finished reviewing some notes for next week's classes. With that out of the way, he intended to devote the rest of evening to the upcoming Athletics Board meeting, the last one of the semester. He knew that the football problem would be *the* subject—he had better be ready.

His mind-set had changed since he read Rory's detailed report about the cheating issue. There were some sleepless nights as he accepted a problem he had denied or, at best, ignored for years. Yes, WKU football players were different. They acted differently and were treated differently than the rest of the student body. He had connected the dots: there was a broad academic gap between regular students and many athletes—unfair for both. He realized that he always knew this, but he obviously had wanted football so badly that he ignored that difference. He found himself asking the now obvious question, "Where in the hell have I been?"

Mike worked hard to keep an open mind, carefully analyzing the football issue as he would a technical problem in computer engineering. When he added the current football players' infractions to his own experiences and to his knowledge of the state of the sport across the country, the conclusions were stark: There were serious flaws in the generally held opinions of the merits of a nationally competitive university football team—flaws that had left the nasty scar of academic failure on many former players. Yes, the football program at WKU was in trouble—trouble that cast a long shadow over the real purpose of the university.

18.

Howling wind, lightning, crashing thunder, and pouring rain outside Tower Hall was appropriate for the last Athletics Board meeting of the spring semester. The group was somber as Chair Rory Kabat reviewed the results of the investigation of the cheating incident.

Fifteen football players had conspired with three undergraduate students who worked as assistants in the university computer center to break into university files and alter records containing critical test and grade information. Furthermore, substantial amounts of money had changed hands. Suspension, expulsion, and even criminal charges were being considered for those involved. The team could lose a substantial fraction of its championship football roster.

There were mixed reactions from board members. The Athletics director, Tim Barnes, stood with a handful of notes in his hand. He was nervous, wearing a forced smile. Barnes glanced at his paperwork and then looked up at the chairman. "Professor Kabat, you and I have been on this board for quite a while. I—we—have seen many problems come and go. Regarding this latest upheaval, I think you will agree with me that it is critical that we keep things in perspective."

The room was exceptionally quiet as Barnes continued speaking, "These things happen. Athletics at this university and any other that I know of are far from perfect. Yes, this problem is on a larger scale than we have seen previously, but it will pass. By the time we are finished here, we may lose a few players"—he paused, looking around the table, shaking a finger at his listeners—"but our football team with its great tradition will continue to be strong."

Barnes's comments drew scattered applause. A notable exception was Professor Ellen Martin. A usually quiet participant, she suddenly slapped her hands on the table and stood abruptly, responding sharply to Barnes, "Director Barnes! If you have read the same reports I have, it should be crystal clear that this is *not* a 'these things happen' incident!"

Martin had recently stepped down as chair of the Chemistry Department. Her reputation was based on outstanding teaching skills, a fine research record, and her success as a manager. The Athletics Board had already experienced many benefits of her organizational skills.

Her comments at board meetings were usually limited, but she did her homework. Her quietly stated questions and suggestions were always well-thought-out and to the point. On this day, her angry reaction seemed to stun many of the members.

Pointing her finger at Barnes, she spoke sharply, "This fiasco is the result of a sophisticated attempt by a significant number of people— *football* people—to rupture the academic learning process. It reflects on *all* members of our university community. We must deal with it *now!*"

Barnes snapped back, "The problem with you academics is that you do not understand the role of a successful NCAA Division I football team in a modern university."

Mike Wolf was suddenly on his feet, raising his voice to be heard above the clamor around the conference table, "May I speak?"

Kabat raised a hand to silence the loud exchange between Barnes and Martin. Nodding to Mike, he said, "You have the floor, Dr. Wolf."

"In case some of you don't know it, I am a former student of Kansas Western. I played football here under the present coach who, incidentally, recommended that I be appointed to this board."

He cleared his throat and paused to sip some water from his paper cup. "Seeing the football program as both a player and now as a faculty member, I think I am qualified to make some observations."

Mike spoke calmly and confidently, "There is no doubt in my mind that we have a very serious situation here. I agree with Professor Martin, this is something that cannot be put off.

"We know that the offending students will be dealt with by the administration. This board's responsibilities are to identify the root cause of the problem and propose effective solutions so it doesn't happen again. "I don't think we can accomplish these tasks in the remaining hour or so of this meeting."

Professor Kabat looked around the table at the now silent members. "Well said, Professor Wolf. Since this is our last scheduled meeting for the spring semester, I will ask one or two of you to join me occasionally to work on this over the summer. Beginning now, questions, suggestions, and constructive criticisms are invited. You know my email address.

"Our goal will be to present our final conclusions and recommendations to the university community at the first general faculty meeting of the fall semester. Any problems with that plan?"

A motion was made to accept Professor Kabat's proposal. After unanimous approval, the meeting was adjourned.

Mike was putting his notes into his briefcase when Rory Kabat asked him to stay around for a few more minutes. "Mike, I want to thank you for your suggestion to step back to deal more thoughtfully with the football problem. You defused a bad situation. The comments flying around were getting pretty nasty."

Mike nodded. "I think I might be learning something here. Glad I could help."

Kabat replied, "It turns out that I need some more help from you. What would you think about meeting with me a few times over the summer to work out a solution to this football mess? We could bounce our ideas off the rest of the board by email with a goal of finalizing our response by the end of the summer."

Mike closed his eyes and rubbed his forehead for a couple of seconds as some competing images flashed across his mind's eye: fall lecture and lab preps and research responsibilities versus the faces of Tank Kozlowski and Ray Smith.

Refocusing his attention on Rory Kabat, he sensed that something important was about to happen here—he was needed. "Sure, Professor Kabat, whatever I can do to help."

Kabat reached out to shake Mike's hand, adding, "Given our task and our likely time together, I think you had better call me Rory."

Rory Kabat and Mike Wolf met with President Summerville a week later to discuss their preparation of the board's formal response to the football problem. After a cordial welcome, Mike quickly found himself sitting on the edge of a very serious conversation. Jane Summerville was adamant. "There is no doubt in my mind that this situation is critical. We have a major task to complete in the next couple of months." She paused.

"There are two goals. We must publicly condemn these infractions and"— she pounded her fist on the desk and raised her voice—"we must ensure that they never happen again, ever!

"Certainly, I will have the final say, but I will depend on your detailed knowledge of the sport and feasible ways to fix it. I want no surprises. I am as close as email."

Ten minutes later, Mike and Rory walked across the campus. The wide blue Kansas sky with a few scattered clouds on the horizon offered them a pleasant, brief distraction. Silent for a few minutes, they were each considering what the president's assignment meant for the rest of their summer.

Mike glanced over at his boss.

Kabat, now in his early seventies, still carried himself as the army officer he was in Vietnam. A solid five feet ten, he dressed more formally than his younger colleagues, usually in a suit and tie. His bald pate only emphasized his intense, no-nonsense stare whenever he engaged someone in conversation. Close to retirement, he had literally given his all to the university as a professor and an able administrator.

They stopped briefly for a few words before going to their separate offices. Rory looked somberly at his assistant. "This assignment is going to be tough, Mike. We have a very busy summer ahead of us. The pressure will be on in more ways than you probably expect.

"Today, I got word that the local media are now asking questions about the cheating fiasco. I wouldn't be surprised that they have been given a heads-up by one of the town representatives on the board—they will soon be in our faces. More than a little premature, but we have to be ready to deal with it."

Rory stopped for a few seconds and gazed skyward. Rubbing his bare head, he smiled ironically. "I think a bad thunderstorm with a lot of wind, rain, and hail and even a tornado or two would be easier to deal with than this mess.

"As far as the press and the TV talking heads are concerned, we don't want to speak to them prematurely. Our recommendations to the president have not been finalized. Even after we complete them and advise her, the final official word must first come from her office. Just be aware that the media folks will continue to push us for information that we don't have or can't give to them." He smiled at Mike. "My best advice in dealing with them is to be nice, but be firm—don't hesitate to say 'No comment.'"

19.

Rory Kabat met Mike a couple of times a week during late June to generate a rough outline of their report to the faculty. The warm days lent themselves to informality. Rory shed his jacket and tie, and Mike relaxed in jeans and a T-shirt.

Mike contributed some useful ideas and editorial comments, but his primary tasks involved searching for reports related to cheating incidents among athletes at other institutions and to consider the reactions and current policies of those schools. He felt like a graduate student again, spending hours on the web digging out information.

A gradual change in Rory's schedule began in mid-July. He called for fewer meetings. Mike was relieved at first—but he knew that if he was really going to help Rory prepare, they needed more discussion about the data he was digging up. On the other hand, his fieldwork was producing some interesting results, and more of his evenings were being spent reviewing those data as well as class and lab preparations for the fall semester.

Mike sat at his kitchen table late on a warm July evening. He had just completed the conclusions section of a project report. That work had gone well with the development of an algorithm to simplify the transfer and analysis of wind data from remote instrument sites. If his reviewers found his work as good as he thought it was, another round of funding would be in order.

He sat back from his computer screen and stretched and yawned. He was done early for a change. Thoughts of a relaxing evening crept into his head—watching some mindless TV or, maybe for a change, going to bed early. He laughed at the idea. *What a concept—more sleep!*

The buzz of his smartphone brought him back to reality. Mike's reaction at the sound of Laura's voice defined a happy guy. "Hey, biologist, I was just thinking about giving you a call!"

She laughed. "Well, here I am. I beat you to the draw!"

Laura had been as busy as Mike. After a successful four-week summer cruise off the North Carolina Coast, she was now back on campus, where her days were spent analyzing data and honing her own classes for the upcoming semester. Since her return, their so-called social life had been limited to a few moments over an occasional cup of coffee or when their paths crossed in the library.

Lately, Laura had found herself thinking about her colleague Michael. No, she reasoned, *colleague* doesn't cut it. Maybe *friend*? Maybe more? She would shake her head talking to herself, "C'mon, girl, none of that stuff. No time!"

They enjoyed a relaxing chat about the weather, the rapid passage of summer, and a word or two about their respective course preparations. Finally, they agreed to meet the next evening for a walk to Benny's, a local restaurant that was easy on the pocket-books of new faculty.

Mike had barely returned to his report when there was another call— Rory Kabat's wife.

"Hi, Mike."

"Mrs. Kabat, good to hear your voice."

"Mike, Rory would like to meet with you concerning his presentation of the Athletics Board report. He is a bit concerned about the time. The general faculty meeting is only a month away, and he says that there is still much to do. Would you mind dropping by here tomorrow to speak with him?"

Without hesitation, Mike replied, "Sure, Mrs. Kabat, I can. What time? Ten a.m.? I'll be there."

The fact that Kabat's wife called rather than Rory himself worried Mike. He wondered about Kabat's health, hoping that the situation wouldn't get worse.

It got worse.

The next morning, Mike was about to leave for Kabat's home when a call on his iPhone stopped him at the door. It was Rory's wife again. Her concern was apparent. "Rory and I are here at the hospital. He had some sort of heart incident this morning. The doctor said that it is not life- threatening, but he will be in the hospital for at least another week and then will need some extended rest at home. The doctor was adamant—Rory is to have absolutely no stress during that period."

Mrs. Kabat paused for a few seconds then quietly explained further, "Unfortunately, his doctor's orders mean he cannot participate in any way in Athletics Board business. As I understand it, the vice chair Professor Ellen Martin will take over. I hope you understand."

Mike assured her that he and the rest of the members could handle it. He asked a few questions about Kabat's situation—and how was she doing? Could he help with anything? Mrs. Kabat thanked him warmly, assuring him that she was OK and had plenty of assistance.

Mike stood for a minute, phone in hand, when the call was over. He closed his eyes and digested the impact of his suddenly changing responsibilities at the upcoming general faculty meeting. His voice echoed off his kitchen cabinets, "Who will make Rory's presentation? Ellen Martin doesn't know any detail about the football thing. That will be tough on her. What a shitty situation!"

Early the next morning, Mike was at work in his office when the insistent sound of his smartphone interrupted him. It was Ellen Martin. The president wanted to meet with them to discuss Kabat's situation and the pending presentation on the cheating issue at the general faculty meeting, now only a few weeks away.

Twenty minutes later, Ellen and Mike were escorted into Summerfield's office by her secretary. Neither had any idea whether Rory's—now Ellen's— planned presentation to the faculty would be significantly modified or even canceled.

Jane Summerville sat on the edge of her chair with her clasped hands on the desktop. She immediately got to the point. They must go ahead with the football report. "This issue is too important for the university. Much incomplete information has gotten out to the press, and the possibility of misinterpretation is large. We must publicly state WKU's standing on the entire issue and be absolutely clear on what solutions are being considered."

Then she dropped a presidential bomb. "Professor Wolf, I am comfortable with you making the presentation."

Mike blinked and opened his eyes wide in surprise.

The president continued, "You are a former athlete at WKU, you know the coaching staff, and most importantly, you have worked closely with Chairman Kabat." Nodding to Ellen Martin, she said, "I also have the recommendation from the acting chairman that you should present your findings. Ellen, do you wish to add anything?"

Martin reached over and put her hand on Mike's back. "I totally agree. Rory Kabat and this man have been the leads on this issue until Rory became ill. Mike knows the problem better than any of us. He should make the presentation on the football issue to the faculty. The board's response to the university community cannot be put off.

"Mike, I will certainly be available to work with you on any last-minute questions and preparations. I have no doubt that your presentation will go well."

Mike sat quietly, listening carefully, his hands on his knees. Beads of sweat on his forehead belied his apparent calmness.

Jane Summerville began putting papers in her briefcase. It was clear the meeting was at an end. Checking her watch, she said, "I have an appointment with the faculty of the History Department in about ten minutes, I'd better be on my way."

Smiling at Mike, she said, "This shouldn't be too difficult, Professor Wolf. Just remember that all you need to do is to summarize the problem and outline the possible solutions that you and Rory have hammered out. Nothing more. Keep it short and to the point. I will be traveling quite a bit between now and then, but I can be reached by email."

A few minutes later, Mike and Ellen Martin stepped out into the sunlight. At first, there was no conversation as they both absorbed Mike's assignment. His anxiety was obvious. He gritted his teeth and shook his head. "Well, this could make some interesting headlines." He laughed nervously. "I can see them now: *Junior Professor Falls on His Face.*"

Ellen spoke quietly, "Mike, I think that Jane has made the right decision. I'm sure that you can do this. And I can help. Please contact me anytime."

They shook hands and then walked off to their respective offices.

Mike attempted to digest his new situation. He needed some time by himself, time to think. A glance at his watch told him he had about a half hour before his next appointment. He detoured from the path and walked across a grassy knoll toward Arnold Stadium—a good place to think about football for a few minutes.

He passed through the open gates and slowly climbed the steps up to an entrance into the arena. He paused, gazing at the empty place. The only sound was the wind. His thoughts were roiling.

Mike sat down and leaned forward, his head in his hands. He would much rather be cracking heads out there as a football player than dealing with his new assignment. Suddenly, he stood up and yelled loudly at the vacant place, "Damn, damn, damn! It's me—I'm the one who will give the presentation to the whole goddamn university. Me! Oh my god!"

After some more headshaking and teeth-gritting, the old "last play of the game" attitude crept into his consciousness, eliciting another loud comment, "Quit crying, you jerk. It's tough, but you can do it!" He gritted his teeth and growled to himself, "Just do it . . . and do it right!"

Assistant Professor Wolf's problems multiplied in the next few days. Rory's wife gathered his notes for the planned presentation and had them delivered to Mike's office. Mike was confounded. Despite their earlier discussions, Rory's material was scattered and incomplete—strong evidence that something was taking its toll on his concentration before his health problems became obvious. It would take Mike hours just to organize Rory's notes with many gaps to fill. The pressure was on in more ways than he could have imagined.

20.

ate on Thursday afternoon, Mike had just left his office. It had been an exceptionally busy day, and he was happy to be outside soaking up some great weather. It was late August—still summer—but a few yellow leaves were already tumbling out of the trees.

He took advantage of the informality of the last days before classes began, dressed casually in an old pair of khaki shorts, running shoes, and an ancient T-shirt decorated with a faded Kansas City Royals logo. An old baseball cap shaded his eyes as he headed toward the west side of the campus and the lowering sun. With a knapsack slung across his shoulder, he appeared to be just another one of the many students pouring onto campus for the start of classes.

He went through a mental checklist as he walked, a reflection of the detailed list on his computer screen back in the office— lab organization done, computer setups rechecked, and lecture material revised. He had even found time to edit a draft of his latest journal article. Despite the satisfaction with the completion of those tasks, he was dragging a bit— the limp was more pronounced—and he was hungry. And there was his major concern: his presentation on the football issue at the general faculty meeting was the next day—he had a long evening ahead of him.

He stepped into his small living room and tossed his cap onto a chair. He paused for a second, shaking his head at the random stacks of used paper coffee cups and empty take-out boxes scattered among books and class notes for the new semester. What a mess. But cleanup would have to wait.

Three of the four chairs surrounding the kitchen table were loaded with Athletics Board material. And that didn't include the files and notes on his computer and his smartphone. Shaking his head at the sight, Mike thought, *Welcome to Athletics Board Central!*

He lowered himself into the one empty chair and put his elbows on the table with his face in his hands. He was worried. Tomorrow's meeting was a big deal, and he had better do a good job. But he was tired. The words *just for a second* went through his mind as he leaned over the desk with his head on his folded arms. He slept heavily—and dreamed.

Mike sat on Professor Kabat's seat at the conference table at an Athletics board meeting. He was a bit confused. Oddly, the table was much longer than usual with the other board members gathered at the far end—at least half a football field away.

He was not alone at his end of the table—he was closely flanked by two very large individuals in bright-red football uniforms and huge helmets. Sweat glistened on the faces of those towering behemoths. He turned awkwardly to his left and looked up to see the empty countenance of Tank Kozlowski. Squirming around to his right, he realized that he was being squeezed by the menacing body of Coach Brady.

Brady's raspy voice fell loudly and threateningly on Mike's ear. "Goddamn it, Wolf! You are one of us! You know us! Kick those academic asses! Save our team! Save our players!"

At the same time, Tank Kozlowski smiled absently while putting a huge arm around Mike's shoulders. He looked vacantly into Mike's face, saying, "Hey, Mike. Saw you walking across campus. Remember, you said that you are going to visit me at home. You can tell me about our football games."

In the hazy distance at the other end of the table, blurry faces of the members of the board chanted, "What are we going to do? What are we going to do?"

A loud bell rang in Mike's ear.

Startled out of his uneasy slumber, he stood suddenly at his kitchen table. A little wobbly and confused, he shook his head, asking himself in a loud voice, "What in the hell is going on?"

The noise was the doorbell. Mike rose stiffly from his chair, almost staggering to throw open his front door. He was pissed off, ready to chase away whoever it was so he could get back to his preparations for tomorrow's meeting.

He opened the door to Laura—an angry Laura.

"And just where in the hell have you been, Professor Wolf?"

"A . . . Laura, hi. Sorry I've been out of touch. Just busy . . . some dicey work on the Athletics Board. Sorry I haven't called. It's good to see you." Laura was mad. She looked up at him, frowning and shaking her smartphone at him. "Michael, all you have to do is text me. Something short like 'Hi—busy.'" Her voice softened. "For some reason, I worry." Suddenly, they were in each other's arms. Kissing passionately. Then, just as quickly, they stepped apart.

He seemed astounded. "What are we doing? You . . . me."

Laura was stunned, a little confused. Putting her hands to her mouth, she whispered, "I'm not sure."

She slowly retreated to the door, apologizing, "Sorry I upset you, Michael. I was just worried."

Mike stood, hands on his hips. He looked down for a moment—then directly into Laura's beautiful brown eyes. "Laura, don't go." He smiled. "That was the nicest thing that has happened to me in . . . in forever!"

He apologized again for being out of touch. "It's just this football mess. Rory Kabat is ill, and the president has asked me to make the presentation at the general faculty meeting in his place. She knows that Rory and I had a lot of critical discussions early this summer and that I have a rough outline of his talk. My problem is that Rory has been too sick to work with me on any of the details. I can't even talk to him about my final preparations."

Laura had thought that, in his junior position on the board, Michael was just helping Rory with some research. But now, the situation sounded more than difficult. The strain on him was obvious.

He nervously put his hands in his pockets, looking over Laura's shoulder as if there was an answer to his dilemma out there somewhere. With an embarrassed shake of his head, he looked at her and apologized again, "Laura, sorry about my behavior. When this damned meeting is over, you can buy me a beer." He laughed. "Better yet, I will buy you two beers!"

The special Laura smile he loved danced across her lips. "I had better go, Professor Wolf. Given this encounter, I would suspect that, in any further discussions, we will not be focusing on work."

Starting to leave, she turned and looked back at him, saying softly, "Michael, that was a very, very special moment"—she tilted her head— "and a wonderful surprise."

Mike whispered to himself as she walked away, "Wow!" Then, slapping himself on the forehead, he exclaimed loudly, "C'mon, Wolf! Focus, focus!" Retreating to his chair at the kitchen table, he stared out of the dark window for thirty seconds then looked back at his preparation for tomorrow's presentation. He had reviewed Rory Kabat's notes several times. Answers to two key questions were clear: What exactly happened?

Who was involved? He could easily deal with those in the first few minutes of his presentation.

It was the president's third assignment that rang in his ears: "Outline the possible solutions you and Rory have hammered out." Unfortunately, Rory's notes didn't give Mike much guidance—he was essentially on his own.

The task was daunting. Mike had to give a clear response to the key question: how should WKU respond to the football crisis to ensure that such a situation never happens again?

Lately, that question had taken on a different, uncomfortable form in Mike's mind: *is intercollegiate football a valid university activity in its present form?*

21.

A noisy larger-than-usual crowd poured into the main campus auditorium for the first general faculty meeting of the fall semester. Word was out that the focus of this year's meeting would be on the football cheating issue. Faculty members, students, alumni, and many others jammed the seats. Local newspaper, TV, and radio reporters were present, and there were rumors that members of the national press were also there. Auditorium doors were closed when people began to stand in the side aisles. Latecomers had to watch the proceedings on closed-circuit TV screens in the entrance hall.

Onstage, the scheduled speakers sat on chairs arranged behind the podium: President Summerville, Athletics Director Tim Barnes, acting Athletics Board Chair Ellen Martin, and Assistant Professor Mike Wolf. The crowd quieted down as the president rose and approached the lectern. She opened with a welcome for the new school year and her usual general report on Western Kansas University. As optimistic and informed as her words were, they blew by most of the audience, most of whom had come only to hear about one thing—the football problem.

Athletics Director Tim Barnes spoke next. He opened with a summary of the status of all sports programs, emphasizing the potential for WKU's success in upcoming football season. He briefly addressed the cheating, condemning the behavior of "a few errant players," emphasizing that "these are isolated incidents that have been blown out of proportion. Believe me, from my position as director of athletics, I know we have the situation under control."

A reporter in the front row of the audience raised her hand to be recognized by Barnes. Such question-and-answer exchanges were unusual at these meetings, and Barnes was confused for a second. With a silent question on his face, he looked back at the president.

She nodded. Barnes turned to the reporter, "Go ahead."

She asked, "Can you give us some more details about the rule violations and the expected consequences for the athletes involved?"

With a deep sigh, Barnes answered the question for what seemed to him to be the hundredth time. "In general, I can say that the violations involve cheating on a series of examinations by a group of football players. Details will be made available when appropriate."

A cacophony of questions and comments erupted from the floor. John Roach, a nonvoting board member representing the local business community, stood and waved his hand for recognition.

He spoke loudly, "Ladies and gentlemen, I suggest that we keep these incidents in proper perspective." He smiled, spreading his arms. "Yes, a few rules were broken by a few players"—he shook his head and laughed at his own words—"feeling their oats, so to speak. That is really a nonissue. The coaches will handle those problems. It is the overall football program that is important here. For years, we have had winning teams, which have brought enormous national recognition to this institution. Have no doubt that we will get beyond these isolated infractions and secure our reputation for our athletics accomplishments—especially for WKU football."

Tim Barnes applauded and nodded, thanking Roach for his support.

There were several verbal reactions from the audience. A scattering of spectators jumped to their feet and shouted contrasting opinions.

"Western Kansas Prairie Dogs rule! Football forever!"

"Don't whitewash these violations! They are serious! You are wrong!" Barnes stepped aside as President Summerville came forward, obviously feeling obliged to make a few calming statements. A tall woman in her late fifties, her resonant voice stifled all other comments, "I remind everyone that Western Kansas University's official position on this situation has not yet been released. Today, the recommendations of the Athletics Board will be presented. I will make the final decision after the Academic Senate has reviewed those recommendations and advised me.

"In the meantime, I remind you that this is a university—a center for reasoning and mindful discussion. I ask you to leave your stadium behavior in the stadium!"

The cessation of background noise was instantaneous.

Ellen Martin moved to the microphone. "This board's analysis of the football problem was supposed to be presented by its chairman, Professor Rory Kabat. Unfortunately, he is ill. I am the acting chairman in his absence.

"I want to make it clear that Professor Kabat has personally requested that Assistant Professor Mike Wolf make today's presentation. Professor Wolf has worked closely with him on this matter." She turned and nodded to Mike.

He walked to the podium to scattered applause. It seemed like a mile to him until he finally stepped up to the microphone. Out of the corner of his eye, he saw some engineering faculty who sat together near the front of the audience, smiling and applauding politely. But that support disappeared quickly when a reporter in the front row leaned over to a colleague, speaking loud enough for Mike to hear, "This guy looks like he is still in graduate school. What the hell does he know?"

Mike turned to his notes, trying to ignore the comment and its source. He knew that he was as ready as he would ever be. He had given plenty of presentations to tough audiences at engineering conferences. How could this be different?

It was different. His heart was beating rapidly, and his hands shook as he placed his laptop on the lectern and turned it on. He took a sip of water to relieve a very dry mouth and began, "I want to begin my presentation with a wish for the speedy recovery of my colleague and mentor, the chair of the Athletics Board, Professor Rory Kabat.

"Over the last couple of months, Professor Kabat and I carefully examined the evidence for, and the impact of, the ill-advised behavior of some of our football players. The results—"

A voice from the back of the hall called out, "Can you please speak up?" Embarrassed, Mike leaned toward the microphone and raised his voice, "The results of our investigation are on firm ground. We know what happened. We know who was involved.

"By the way, in case you aren't aware, I'm a second-year assistant professor in the Department of Computer Engineering and an alumnus of this institution. My other relevant experience includes three seasons as a halfback on WKU's football team. I have been a member of the Athletics Board for a year."

The audience increased its chatter, reflecting briefly on Mike's background. Then they settled down to listen.

He continued, relaxing into his best classroom lecture mode—logic and clarity were his hallmarks. "The press has made the cheating episode common knowledge, although some of their details aren't quite right. To clarify, twenty-six football players—roughly a third of the current team roster—stole exams and manipulated grades over a period of at least two semesters. They paid for the help of four student technicians from the university computer center. We know this is true. An appropriate university reaction is already underway according to university regulations and applicable state laws."

The restless crowd considered the charges against the players with several separate discussions springing up across the auditorium. Mike's voice became noticeably stronger, quieting the room. "The questions we must answer as a faculty go beyond who did what? How did they do it? And what are the short-term consequences? We already know most of those details. There are two more important questions: What is it in our collective football mentality that allowed this event to happen? And what must we do to prevent it from happening again?"

Many in the audience were caught off guard. They had expected a brief discussion of the cheating incident followed by the usual upbeat preseason cheerleading session. Not so. Audible reactions spread across the room.

Wolf raised his voice, silencing the chatter. He now spoke without notes. "Personally, I believe that there are certain aspects of football that contribute to the development of an individual in a very positive way. Football teaches leadership and teamwork. Football helps a player understand the importance of self-discipline, persistence, and hard work. And beyond the field, both in the stadium and through the media, football provides entertainment for many fans.

"In contrast, this cheating incident has focused on a dark side of the game. It is much more than an embarrassment. It is a warning bell for our university community—a symptom of a deeper problem in our current football program."

He nervously adjusted the position of his laptop and then looked at his audience. "So, what do we do about it? How do we reduce the chances of a similar incident happening in the future? I'm here to lay out some potential answers to that question. But I warn you, none are perfect and some are conflicting."

Mike's words were again met with loud comments from the audience. He paused for a few seconds then continued, "That deeper problem is linked to the fact that, especially over the last forty years, football has become a nearly independent entity on major campuses around the country—ours included."

Head football coach Mitch Anderson and his assistants, seated in the front row center, were visibly surprised at Mike's charge, giving one another frowning glances.

Mike continued, "What has caused this change?

"The one-word answer to that question is money! Football makes money for the university. In fact, at most large universities, including ours, many minor sports such as tennis and swimming are at least partially supported by football revenues. In case you didn't know it, in college sports vernacular, football is often referred to as a revenue-generating sport.

"For a revenue-generating sport to be judged successful, it must—I repeat—*must* win. Winning teams pack stadiums with paying fans. Winning teams bring in TV and advertising money."

Mike paused to take another swallow of water. He looked over the top of the cup at the audience. It was clear that he had their attention. He set his cup down. "The independence of our football program from the traditional goals of WKU is demonstrated with its selection of players. For a team to win, it must recruit top high school and junior college athletes. "I can't give the precise correlation between the academic and athletic performances of recruited football players, but based on my own involvement when I participated in the college football wars and from my more recent experiences as both a faculty member and a member of this board, that correlation is weak at best. Innate football talent does not necessarily equate to academic success. If you doubt this fact, simply compare the graduation rates of our football players with the rest of the student body."

For the first time since he stepped up to the podium, he sensed that his listeners were grasping the importance of his words. Combining the logic of an engineer and the determination of an athlete, he pressed on.

"A meaningful examination of our football program can be made in terms of what this university is supposed to be about."

He looked directly at his audience. "The last time I checked, WKU's purpose is caught up in one word—truth!"

"The truth is that during both the fall season and spring practice, football players have limited study time. They must miss classes and reschedule exams that conflict with travel and games. These interruptions lead to poor academic performance for many players and push some into cheating in an effort to stay eligible, grade-wise."

For a second, the voice of an alum could be heard from the back of the auditorium. "Who do you think you are? You—" The rest of his words were lost in noisy discussions that spread through the audience.

Mike waited for the clamor to dissipate. "The truth is that, too often, football players are considered second-class citizens. Many faculty and students outside athletics view the student part of the student-athlete label to be false. They only see football players as marginal students who receive special privileges.

"The truth is that given the pressure on those athletes to be successful football players, those special privileges are really not so special. Many will argue that a so-called athletic scholarship is a major benefit for football players. The truth is that it is poor pay for a tough job.

"Have any of you ever stopped to consider that a successful university football player is required to engage successfully in *two* demanding tasks? He must perform well on the football field *and* in the classroom. That double requirement does not exist for most other students."

The audience's reaction to Mike's statement increased with louder comments coming from all corners of the auditorium.

He ignored the noise and continued, "Those are the truths. The problem facing us today goes much deeper than the recent player incidents. The real question that must be answered is, Can this institution—can we—do anything to stop the football 'tail' from wagging the university 'dog?'"

Mike had their attention. He was adamant. "Yes, there are solutions. But I warn you, each of them will require some thoughtful and courageous decisions.

"Here are three possibilities. The first is that we simply proceed as usual to prepare for the next football season. This would mean accepting the loss of about a third of the current players due to their involvement in the cheating scheme." He paused. "*And* it would also include the loss of some players who just don't want to play for a team with problems. Otherwise, next fall's football season would start as usual."

Mike paused to let the audience absorb his first proposal.

Mitch Anderson stood, looking around at the audience and then up at Mike. "Professor Wolf, understand that we can't simply throw away players. Certainly, some guys made bad choices, but they are young. Young people make mistakes. And they are some of our best ball players! Is this cheating thing any reason to decimate the team? We shouldn't kick them out. Give them a break!"

Mike looked up at the audience. "Those excuses don't go very far. This is a serious academic problem—the worst that any WKU team has ever experienced. As far as the university rules against cheating are concerned, I don't make those. The university does. The culprits in this case have been identified. They must suffer the consequences, regardless of my—or your—opinions.

"If we cannot tolerate the certain weakening of our team, there is another possibility for a long-term solution. That is, WKU could step away from Division AA football for a few seasons to allow the impact of this extensive cheating episode to be absorbed. In a sense, football would be de-emphasized at WKU.

"If you are unfamiliar with that term, *de-emphasis*, check your sports history books. De-emphasis was attempted by a significant number of universities more than sixty years ago. At the time, they felt that football was at odds with the goals of higher education.

"What happened? The concept of free substitution was dropped. In some leagues, the season was shortened, and even spring practice was eliminated.

"Ultimately, in most leagues, de-emphasis lost favor and was dropped. I remind you of that period because today, for WKU, the need for de- emphasis has returned as a ghost from the past. From a practical point of view, WKU might consider temporary de-emphasis—to keep the football tradition alive while dealing with the very serious current problems. At some point in the future, a return to the top NCAA division could be considered.

One audience member stood and shouted at Mike, "No way! You are wrong, Wolf! Leave Prairie Dogs' football alone!"

Mike was quick to respond: "I am not telling you what to do. I'm simply reminding you that WKU football has a bad problem. The important question is, How do we solve it and still save Prairie Dogs' football?

"The answer to this question won't be found by throwing our hands up and yelling at each other and hoping for the best—it requires that we put our heads together to produce a viable solution. My suggestion of temporary de-emphasis is one short-term possibility. If you think you have a better idea, bring it to the table."

Mike spoke clearly and confidently, "To find a real permanent solution, we must bring in other universities who recognize the same problem. We must collaborate with those who are willing to consider some major changes in the way college football is conducted these days. No, we can't do it alone, but we certainly can start the conversation."

Yes, there were several options to cure the recent cheating ills, but Mike had pushed beyond any short-term fix to address the deeper cause. The hall rumbled with discussions and arguments.

In the back of the auditorium, a person leaning against the wall at the end of the center aisle had one hand covering one ear and a phone in the other. Mike recognized him as a sports reporter from the *Gardnerville Gazette*. Another person in the third row had a smartphone in her hand, texting rapidly.

Assistant Coach Brady talked intently to Mitch Anderson, pointing repeatedly and angrily at Mike. In contrast with Brady's behavior, Anderson maintained his coaching posture, control, and intense focus seen so often on the sidelines at critical moments in WKU football games.

Brady suddenly slapped his hand loudly on the arm of his chair, shouting, "You've gone too far, Wolf! Take your crazy ideas and get out of here!"

Looking directly at the faces of the audience, Wolf asked, "Where do we stand on this issue? What are we going to do about this national problem that is *here now* on our doorstep? Do we follow? Or do we *lead*? Your call."

The audience was quiet, digesting Mike's comments.

Catcalls began. "You are wrong! Kansas Western has a long wonderful football tradition, and you have denigrated it."

"Hey, *Assistant* Professor, you had better get a little experience before you talk about these ridiculous big ideas!"

"Where did this guy come from? He can't be an alum!"

Just then, in the back of the auditorium, Mike saw Laura. As their eyes met, she stood and began to applaud, slowly at first. Her lead was followed by others. The applause grew louder with encouraging shouts across the hall. Mike saw members of his own department, standing, clapping, waving, clenching their fists, and shouting their support.

A grim Mitch Anderson was joined by Tim Barnes as he walked out. They both looked up at Mike as they passed the podium, shaking their heads in consternation. They were followed by Ralph Bennett, John Roach, and Coach Brady—faces contorted, shaking fists, and mouthing inaudible, but obviously angry, words.

The applause from the large audience that remained in the auditorium lasted several minutes. Mike finally retreated into the wings of the stage, a bit overwhelmed. Soaked in sweat, he wearily shook his head in disbelief that it was over. Looking up, he saw President Summerville standing a few steps away.

She raised her voice to be heard above the clamor, "Be in my office tomorrow morning at eight. We have to talk."

22.

Mike awoke early the next day. It had taken a while for him to get to sleep, but when he finally dozed off, and slept hard. He stretched and rubbed his eyes. He suddenly sat up in bed. "Oh shit! Classes! I'm not ready!" He shook his head and focused, slapping his forehead. "It's Saturday! Mike, you jerk, relax!"

Rolling out of bed, he stumbled into the kitchen. Coffee. He needed coffee.

When the pot began to make its burbling noises, today's tasks began to run through his head: *There were a couple of glitches in the computer visuals for Monday's lecture in his structural dynamics class. He had a meeting with that new grad student—what's his name? Oh yeah, Ed Payon.*

And there were more he couldn't quite articulate. He was still foggy from the fireworks at the yesterday's board meeting.

A few minutes later, coffee cup in hand, Mike stood talking loudly to his computer as it booted up. "Come on! Come on!" The screen lit up with his always complete to-do list. He mumbled impatiently as he scanned the tasks. *Damn board work. At least that was over with.*

His thoughts were interrupted by a cheerful voice. "Good morning, Michael! Are you talking to yourself?"

Surprised, he stood at the doorway to the living room to see Laura, lying on the living room couch. Her beautiful sleepy eyes told him that she had been there all night.

She giggled. "Nice outfit, Michael!"

Mike suddenly realized that he was standing in his underwear. With an embarrassed "Oops!" he retreated into the bedroom, leaning his head around the doorway as he pulled on a robe. "Uhh . . . well . . . hi, Laura! What are you doing there? Here? Did you sleep here last night?"

She stood, stretching and yawning. "I did indeed, Mr. Famous Football Guy. I thought you might want some company after the uproar at the faculty meeting, so I came over last evening.

"Your front door wasn't quite shut. I opened it a crack and called out. You didn't answer, so I figured that you weren't back yet. I came in and sat down to read the paper and wait.

"Michael, I couldn't believe the sports pages! You sure gave those *Gazette* reporters something to write about!

"After a half hour or so, I heard snoring. I peeked into your room, and there you were, sleeping like the proverbial baby. I finally decided, what the hell!—and curled up on the sofa."

She tucked in her blouse and smoothed some wrinkles in her skirt, giving Mike that Laura smile he found so precious. "I slept very well, I might add."

Eyeing his coffee, she asked, "Is there more of that? I sure could use some."

She stood next to him as he poured a cup for her. "Yesterday's meeting was truly exciting, Michael! I bet it wasn't easy for you. Are you OK?"

Mike nodded. "Yeah, I'm fine now, but last night, when I got back, I was really out of it."

He rubbed his uncombed hair and shrugged his shoulders. "I feel perfectly all right despite the fireworks at yesterday's talk. I'm satisfied. Whatever happens now, I gave those people something to think about."

He smiled and raised his coffee cup. "Here's to the end of my dealings with the football mess! Now I can go back to being an almost-organized engineering prof.

"I'm sorry for getting back on the podium. I guess it'll take a while for me to let it go. What I need now is a nice long, quiet walk with a beautiful biologist." He reached over to her and gently pushed some strands of uncombed hair sleepy hairout of her sleepy eyes. "Interested?"

Laura gently pushed his hand away and laughed. "You do go on, Mr. Engineer. How about—"

He interrupted, slapping his hand to his head. "What time is it? Geez, I just remembered I have to be in the president's office at eight a.m. to sample the fallout from the meeting!"

Laura put her hand on his arm. "You have plenty of time, Michael. It's just six thirty, and it's only a fifteen-minute walk from here to her office."

His shoulders dropped, and he exhaled. "Yeah, Laura, you are right. I guess I still need to slow down a little after yesterday's show.

"I doubt the meeting will take more than an hour. How about meeting you at ten at your place? We can walk to a late breakfast. Will that work?" "Absolutely." Slipping her shoes on, she picked up her purse and walked to the door. Mike hesitated then followed her, placing a hand on her shoulder, gently turning her around to face him. Their embrace seemed like the most natural thing in the world. He touched her face then kissed her softly. She responded eagerly, pressing her body tightly to his and reaching inside his loose robe to touch his skin.

Mike stepped back, still holding Laura's shoulders. "Uh, Professor Biologist, Ma'am, I don't think I have to tell you anything about where this is leading—except to say biology rules!"

Laura broke up in laughter and reached up to ruffle his hair. She knew she was ready, but . . . "You are so right, Michael. If rainchecks are valid, I want one now!"

They enjoyed their closeness for a few more seconds, then Mike gently pulled away. "I really hate to say it, Professor Sparks, but our boss, President Summerville, awaits me. I'd better clean up."

She picked up her purse and pulled out a brush to run through her hair. She stood on her toes to kiss his cheek and then walked out of the front door into the sunshine.

He watched her until she was out of sight.

Mike found himself wondering how long his meeting with the president would last. He had a quick shower and shave and another hurried cup of coffee. Breakfast could wait.

He really preferred shorts, T-shirt, and sandals on this beautiful Saturday morning, but he dressed a tad more formally for his meeting. Slacks, a collared shirt, a light sports jacket, and dress shoes were the result. At seven thirty, he crossed the quiet campus to his appointment. His limp was a bit more obvious after yesterday's time standing at the podium.

Ellen Martin, standing in for Rory Kabat, was waiting outside the president's door. Aside from her ever-present briefcase, she appeared a little less businesslike than usual, casually dressed in a pair of jeans, sandals, a white blouse, and light-blue sweater that complemented some early streaks of gray in her black hair.

Ellen and Mike were quite relaxed in each other's company despite differences in their age and academic experience. She had been impressed by Mike's organized efforts and passion to set things right in WKU football. She shook his hand, giving him a friendly smile. "Well, here we are again, Mike. I think it was Yogi Berra who made the classic remark that covers this situation. 'It ain't over . . .'"

Mike nodded. "Yeah, I know . . . till it's over."

Ellen knocked on the office door. Since it was Saturday, the president's secretary wasn't present, and the door was opened by Jane Summerville. Clearly in her weekend attire, she was still dressed a little more formally than her visitors—a light-blue silk blouse, a pair of dark linen slacks, and low heels. An understated pearl necklace and earrings complemented her outfit. She greeted her visitors with handshakes as they stepped inside her spacious office.

President Summerville's large mahogany desk was occupied by a neat stack of newspapers on one side and a PC with a very large screen on the other. Behind her, two more computers with equally large displays filled a long table. Mike identified the equipment as state of the art and marveled at its organization—if only his own work space could be so neat.

Jane invited her visitors to take a seat as she pulled a copy of the *Gazette* from a stack of newspapers on a corner of her desk. She glanced at Mike. "Well, Dr. Wolf, you certainly didn't wear sheep's clothing yesterday. That was quite a show."

Mike colored a bit at the compliment, smiling and nodding his thanks. "You outlined the problem and suggested some potential solutions that, I have to say, really upset the Athletics Department, the football coaches, the players, and many students, as well as some community supporters of WKU football. That is not a criticism. Despite the headache I have from the fallout from your statements, I think that you were right on. I compliment you for an organized, well-thought-out description of our problem—a problem that we must solve."

Ellen Martin agreed. "Yes, Mike, you explained the realities of the football situation and put them in the face of the university community—in my mind, it was about time."

Mike's eyes were on Jane Summerville as Ellen made her remarks. He thought, *Ellen and I know what we think, but Summerville's the boss, and the buck stops at her desk.* He took a deep breath, wondering what was next.

The president clasped her hands as she rested her elbows on the arms of her chair. She looked directly at Mike. "Yes, you spelled out the problem. Now comes the hard part—we have to deal with it."

Tapping the stack of newspapers, she asked, "Have either of you looked at any of these or seen the local news on TV this morning?"

Neither had.

She handed the morning edition of the *Gazette* to Mike. "Read this." Ellen looked over his shoulder at the headline: "WKU Professor Tackles Football Problems."

Inside, the accompanying article was more specific: "Controversial Solution Proposed for WKU Football Program."

"There's more. The local TV station also reported on your talk yesterday. I recorded it on my smartphone. Listen to this."

She played the recording of the lead statement of the commentator. "Yesterday, at the general faculty meeting at WKU, an

Athletics Board member strongly condemned the WKU football program. The backlash was immediate as coaches and many attendees loudly protested."

Mike raised his eyebrows in surprise at the impact of his presentation. The president set her smartphone aside, watching his reaction for a moment. Then she said, "Several of the media's talking heads have focused on those opposed to your solutions. So far, I have neither seen nor heard anything about the positive reactions—but I know there are plenty. Have you been contacted?"

Mike shook his head. He had not.

She went on, "I have already received requests for interviews from a couple of national TV networks and an East Coast newspaper. This is big, and it's getting bigger. You should expect a lot of attention in the next week." Nodding to Ellen, she said, "And don't be surprised if your cell phone starts buzzing too.

"My advice to both of you is to make yourselves available when you can, but don't let this interfere with your academic duties. I will speak to your department chairs.

"Ellen, you have a tough job with Rory still out of the picture. I expect you and Mike to be in touch with each other to maintain a consistent response to the media. Keep me in the loop. I prefer email."

Mike and Ellen were both in deep thought as they walked across the campus after the meeting. The fine weather contradicted the storm of controversy Mike's speech had brought on. They stopped to chat for a few minutes in the sunshine, speculating on what was next, then headed off in separate directions.

Hands in his pockets, Mike ambled slowly back toward Laura's place. The squabble of a flock of crows in a nearby tree brought a smile to his lips. The noise reminded him of the aftermath of last Friday's meeting.

He reached Laura's door and tapped softly. She opened it, immediately seeing the worry in his eyes. She gave him a warm hug and a kiss on the cheek. "Michael, you look a little stressed—a bad meeting?"

He relaxed a bit in her warmth, shaking his head. "No, not bad. Just a little intense. We looked at some of the press's reactions to the meeting." He smiled. "Frankly, I'm glad to be a young relatively healthy junior faculty member. Otherwise, I think I would be dealing with ulcers over this football thing.

"The press has had a field day over my speech. The president's advice— really her warning—was 'Stand by, there's more to come!'"

Laura reached up and touched his face. "My football guy— when you jump out of the huddle, you do go all out!"

Mike frowned, saying quietly, "Beautiful Laura, can we not talk about football for a while?"

"Oh, Michael, I'm sorry. I promise—no more football stuff." She put her hand in his and, with a smile, asked, "Where do we eat?"

She watched him purse his lips with a finger to his chin— another Michael-thinking pose. He nodded. "Ahh, I know. Let's drive to Eddie's Diner near the theater on the other side of town. The place is far enough away from the university to give us a quiet breakfast. He looked at his watch. "Better make that brunch. I bet you're hungry!" Later, as they were enjoying a postmeal coffee, Mike sat back, smiling at Laura. "Can you believe it? We have been here for almost an hour, and there has been absolutely no reference to football by us or anyone else." He lifted his cup in a toast. "Here's to more quiet moments! And especially, here's to more quiet moments with my"—he winked at her—"with my biology friend."

Laura gave him a soft punch on the arm. "Michael, sometimes I think you need lessons in romantic small talk!"

"Aww, I know I'm clumsy when I try that stuff, but you know my heart is in it, don't you?"

She nodded, laughing at his feigned awkwardness. "You are something, my football friend—really something!

"Silliness aside—if you can tell me—how was your meeting with the president?"

The waitress cleared away their dishes. Mike took the opportunity to order another cup of coffee. Laura admonished him, "You drink too much coffee, Professor Wolf."

He laughed at the thought. "Look at it this way—at least it's not whiskey."

Laura gave him an exasperated look. "Tell me about the meeting."

"It was an eye-opener. I know I pushed hard for a solution. I was worried that, maybe, at least to the president, I'd stepped over the line. But no—both she and Ellen Martin supported my contention that WKU football has some serious problems. We considered a next step in dealing with those and with our detractors."

Laura could see some tenseness in Mike's face as he spoke. She suddenly held her hands up. "Time-out, Michael! I really want to hear all the bloody details, but looking at your reappearing worry lines, I'll bet that you are ready to put that stuff away—for today, anyway. So, I'll let you off the hook. Next time is OK."

He reached across to touch her hand. "Laura, you know I tease you about our . . . our relationship. Kidding aside, I want you to know that it is so important to me. You keep me grounded. You listen. You make some wonderful suggestions. You push me to be a better prof. You make me laugh. Just spending these few peaceful minutes with you is—is fantastic!" She held his hand. "Michael, you're right. I have been worried about you—and frustrated. All because I can't help carry the damnable load thrown on you by the Athletics Board. I think you have handled it well, but I know that it has taken a toll."

He wrapped his hands around hers, speaking softly, "Laura, not to worry, you have helped me, really. All of this bad stuff will pass."

They returned to town and parked at Mike's place then walked slowly to Laura's apartment to watch the TV broadcast of the Prairie Dogs' away game. WKU played like it wasn't interested. Mike put his face in his hands then looked up at Laura. "This is horrible. I just can't watch anymore."

She picked up the remote and turned off the TV. "You're right. Our players seem to be sleepwalking. It's pretty bad."

They gave each other a 'what's next?' look. She smiled warmly, whispering, "Michael . . . I . . . Michael, stay with me tonight."

She had said what he was thinking. They stood, facing each other. He put his hands on her shoulders and looked into her eyes. "Laura, you . . ." He shook his head then started again. "Laura, we . . ."

He hesitated again in his frustrated attempt to find the right words . . . the perfect words.

"Romeo, I am not!" He wrapped his arms around her. "Here's my pitch, sweet Laura. I think I have caught that love stuff—and you are it."

He picked her up and carried her into the bedroom.

23.

Mike walked slowly back to his apartment late on Sunday morning. He stepped through his front door more than a little off-balance. No, it wasn't his bad leg—it was the wonderful night with Laura. He had some preparations for his tomorrow's classes, and keeping her sweet countenance out of his thoughts wasn't going to be easy.

He called her. They laughed about the fact that she was also finding that her ability to concentrate, as she laughingly put it, "has been was somewhat compromised."

After chatting for a few more minutes, they agreed that they both had some last-minute classwork hanging over their heads and had better get busy. Mike noticed that her soft "Bye, Michael" seemed to have more words in it than he heard.

Laura and classes aside, football came blasting back into Mike's consciousness when he opened the Sunday edition of the *Gazette*. The front page of the sports section highlighted the Prairie Dogs' game. The two quarters he and Laura had watched at her place were bad, but after they turned the game off, things on the field had gotten worse. In a contest that several preseason pollsters had picked the Prairie Dogs to win, WKU had lost, 6-20. In Coach Mitch Anderson's postgame interview, he referred to "the upsetting events at the general faculty meeting."

A quote from one of the WKU players was more specific, causing Mike to wince as he read it. "Everybody was tired of hearing about the junk that came from Wolf in that faculty meeting last Friday. We had a hard time concentrating on the game."

Mike shook his head as he rolled up the paper and tossed it into the wastebasket. In all his football experience, he had never imagined being the sole cause of a Prairie Dogs' loss. He had always given everything in every play—in every game.

He forced himself to reconnect with the list of tasks on his laptop. He felt a little more organized after an hour or so. He knew the course material well; his lectures were ready to go. His recently revised computer lab was in good shape. New equipment and new software would keep him moving forward. He had to admit, busy as he was, the classwork was still fun and challenging.

* * *

Monday morning, Mike walked into his office to see Jerry Larson, leaning over his laptop. "Wow, Jerry, you are here early! What's up?" is officemate replied angrily, "Ahh shit! This god-dam program worked perfectly last semester, but now, for some unknown reason, it refuses to open. And of course, it's this morning's lecture. "ShitDamn Grrrr!"

Jerry refused Mike's offer to help, continuing to hammer the keys of his laptop. "I made it, I should be able to fix it. It's so damned simple! How could this happen?"

Mike smiled at Jerry's tirade and sat down at his own desk to begin the day's work.

Ten minutes later, Jerry's problem was fixed, and he began to relax. Looking over at Mike, he laughed, shaking his head. "Ahh, that's better. I can't believe I made that stupid mistake. I guess perfection is still a long way off.

"Speaking of perfection, it appears that your Prairie Dogs are still looking for it."

Mike rubbed his never-quite-combed curly hair. "I am on a Prairie Dog sabbatical. At least until the phone rings or the next person knocks on the door."

A knock came with perfect timing. "Come in!" Jerry shouted.

Two students stood in the doorway to introduce themselves as reporters from the WKU *Viewpoint,* the student-run weekly campus newspaper. Mike invited them to sit down, murmuring to Jerry, "What did I just say?"

Jerry excused himself to grab a cup of coffee in the department day room, while Mike moved some chairs around to make room for his visitors in the cramped office space. He welcomed them with a smile. "What's up?" It was hard not to notice that his visitors had a kind of "Mutt and Jeff" look, one a lanky redheaded fellow about six feet three and the other a pudgy, dark-haired guy about five feet five. The semester was just getting underway, and this was probably their first assignment as *Viewpoint* reporters. Obviously nervous, they looked at each other; then the tall reporter gave the other an almost imperceptible nod.

His partner began, "My name is Art Lerner . . . uhh . . . and this is Joe . . . uhh . . . Joe Perry."

Art took a second to compose himself. He crossed and then uncrossed his legs, nervously checking his iPad notes. Clearing his throat, he began, "We'd like to ask you some questions about your presentation at the general faculty meeting last Friday—on the state of WKU football."

Mike checked his watch. "I can give you about thirty minutes. Go ahead."

"Is it true that you want WKU to drop football?"

Mike looked down at his desk for a second. He knew that this was coming, but he wasn't really in the mood to deal with it right now. "That is not exactly true. Were you at the meeting?"

They nodded.

"That's good. Even if you missed something, my presentation is already online, so there is no reason for me to rehash everything. If you recall, my main point was this: WKU football has become a nearly independent operation on campus—more like a business. That status is at odds with the purpose of the university as a place of higher learning.

"The thrust of my presentation was to shine some light on that serious problem. I want to be clear. I asked the questions. Now the university community must provide the answers. It will take time and energy to find a solution that is workable and acceptable to the university community."

The student reporters' fingers danced across their tablets as they continued to take notes, occasionally stopping to ask Mike to repeat a couple of points.

Finally, Art Lerner asked, "What do think will happen, Professor Wolf?"

Mike paused for a few seconds, scratching his head. "I wouldn't want to guess. I suggested a potential solution. I am sure that there are others. They must be examined carefully by all parties. Then we must act decisively—together."

The reporters looked at each other then back at Mike. Jim Perry said, "Thanks for this, Professor Wolf." He hesitated then said, "There is one more thing we want to tell you. We have both spoken with coaches and players. They are a very angry bunch, and many say that if there is a problem with WKU football, it's you."

Nervously, Perry looked again at his partner then at Mike. "I personally have heard threats made by a few ball players—threats of violence."

Unsure of himself, he gave a glance toward the door. "When a couple of them mentioned a specific target, your name came up." He checked his notes and then looked back at Mike. "When I asked them what they really meant by that, they backed off, but I wasn't convinced. I do know that there are some pissed-off people out there. You had better watch your back, Professor."

Mike frowned at the remark. "Hmm. I hadn't really thought much about that." Then he gave a half smile. "Thanks for the warning—I will keep my eyes open."

The two reporters thanked Mike for his time and left him sitting behind his desk considering the caution they had just given to him. He shook his head at the situation, telling himself, *Hell! This is a university. There is always someone who has a different take on things. Those jocks are loud, but they aren't dangerous.*

Mike turned to his computer to open his email for the first time in three days. He found more than a hundred messages since Friday—in fact, 104! Most were responses to his presentation:

"WKU football forever."

"Your football logic doesn't hold water."

"You don't deserve to be a faculty member at this university!"
"Get out before you ruin a long tradition!"

As predicted, a few emails were downright threatening, including some crude epithets. Despite his visitors' warnings just fifteen minutes previously, he decided not to report these cyber-attacks to the campus communications office with the hope that these were just angry students blowing off steam.

Mike's mood was lifted by several messages in support of his presentation. One was from Rory Kabat. *Saw your presentation online. Good Job. BTW, I'm feeling much better. Can have visitors now. Call when you have a moment. Rory.*

He had one lecture later in the morning and a long lab that afternoon. About thirty students were present when he walked into the lecture hall. Mike reflected on the group. *At least no football questions from this bunch.*

The chatter in the room ended as he laid his notes and laptop on the desk. He turned on his projector and looked up at the group. A hand went immediately. Mike nodded to a student who asked with a bit of a grin, "Are we going to talk football, Professor?"

Mike gave an exasperated half smile. "I think that stuff isn't on our schedule today. Stay tuned to the local news for the latest"—he couldn't help himself—"mostly true reports."

The class seemed to relax as Mike began his lecture.

24.

The following morning, Mike returned to his office after his first class. He dropped into his chair with a sigh of relief. His officemate glanced over at him. "Say, Professor Wolf, it strikes me that your energy level has been somewhat sapped with the fireworks of your now famous presentation to the faculty. Am I right, or have you been partying all night?"

Mike smiled at Jerry's effort to relax him. "C'mon, Jer, I don't think I look that bad. That stuff is over, and I'm ready to roar . . . sort of."

Jerry persisted, "I hate to tell you, Mike, but you do look worn out." "Thanks for the concern, Jerry, but another good night's sleep and I will be just fine."

Jerry shook his head as refocused on the material on his desk, mumbling, "We'll see."

Mike pulled out his iPhone to find a message from Ed Johnson requesting a meeting ASAP.

Ten minutes later, he was sitting in Ed's office. Mike's boss was in his lecture mode, pacing nervously behind his desk, hands in pockets, a concerned frown on his face.

"Mike, I think your presentation at the general faculty meeting was right on. I congratulate you for that. It was a long time coming. You certainly put the onus on the university community to clean up its football program. But . . ."

Ed stopped for a moment, looking hard at the young man sitting in front of him. "But there is a downside. As a very busy junior member of this department, you cannot continue in your Athletics

Board mode. Look at yourself. You're a wreck. You're investing way too much time and energy in your board work while trying to keep up with your other duties."

Mike responded, "Ed, I agree that my presentation was a stretch. And yes, I'm a bit tired." He spread his hands pleadingly. "But someone had to step up because of Rory Kabat's health problems. He and I worked on this together. I had to do it. And now it's done."

Mike wanted to stay on the board. He understood how it worked; he knew that he could now operate at a much more relaxed level and still contribute. He looked at Ed. "Rory is better now, and I'm through with the pressure of that one-time presentation."

Ed was clearly dissatisfied with Mike's argument. "If you stay on the board, believe me, your teaching and research efforts will suffer."

He reached for an unlit cigarette, jabbing it into the air to emphasize each point he made. "Yes, I appreciate the fact that you want to do it all— teach, advise, do your research, write your papers—but there is a limit. This board thing is just one too many."

Mike was surprised by Ed's harsh words. He sat forward on his chair to make his case. "C'mon, Ed, I'm OK, I can handle it. I was asked to take over in an unusual situation. It's done. My classes are in good shape. My fieldwork and data analysis are moving along."

Ed shook his head adamantly. He was furious. "Goddammit, Mike, you are *not* OK! You are the center of local and national news. Those damned TV talking heads and reporters are after your butt. I know. This office must have fielded a dozen calls in the last two days—people looking for you. I can't imagine what your email and smartphone activity must be. And believe me, from what I have heard, it's going to get worse!"

Mike could feel his temper rising. He repeated his arguments passionately, "Ed, listen to me! I'm just a junior member of the board. I'm not in charge. The board is working fine under Professor Martin, the acting chair. And Kabat will be back soon. As for me, my classes and research are in good shape—"

Ed interrupted, "No, Mike, you listen to me. I am your boss, and I think that you—we—have reached a breaking point with your Athletics Board assignment."

Ed paused in his pacing and looked over at Mike. He repeated his argument. "You are too new and too busy with teaching, advising, trying to stay on top of your research, and managing your grad students. Yes, your recent presentation to the faculty was . . . was brilliant. You stepped up in an unusual situation and gave your best. Not surprisingly, you stirred up a hornet's nest."

"But I—"

Ed wasn't done. Raising his voice another notch, Mike noticed the secretary had quietly closed Ed's office door. "And now you are fighting off the press. They are requesting interviews galore. I heard that a TV reporter stopped you as you walked out of class, keeping you for at least half an hour—making you late for your office hours!

"And I understand that you also had to cancel a presentation at our weekly seminar series because of a series of telephone calls dealing with the football mess."

"But I—"

"Are these things true?" "Yes, but—"

Ed grasped the edge of desk. He was adamant. "No buts about it. I have informed the president that I want you off that damned time- consuming board!"

Mike remained silent for a few moments, composing himself. He knew his boss was right, but he felt that he hadn't quite finished his job. "What's my drop-dead date?"

"Today. Submit your resignation to the president and the board chairman with a copy to me."

Mike winced. He was surprised at the timing. There were still things he could to do to help Rory. He paused for a few seconds, looking out the window of Ed's office at Tower Hall in the distance, trying to gather his thoughts.

The Computer Engineering Department chairman stood patiently behind his desk with his arms crossed. Finally, Mike looked up, speaking quietly, "OK, Ed. You'll have it within the hour. Sorry to have been such a pain. There was a problem to deal with, and when Rory Kabat got sick, it fell at my feet. I had a responsibility."

Ed sat down and relaxed a bit, smiling at Mike, speaking quietly, "Look, Mike, you are, and will continue to be, an excellent addition to this department. Unfortunately, this football issue and Rory's illness has put you in a position that demands more time than you have. You have handled it as well as—better than—anyone else. Again, I congratulate you for shaking up the university community by laying out the football problem and its potential solution for all of us to consider."

He paused and looked down at his folded hands then looked directly at Mike.

"But now it's over. Your priority is your assignment as an assistant professor in this department. Understood?"

Mike nodded. "Understood."

Patting his bad leg, Mike shook his head with the hint of a smile. "Maybe I'm just an old football player who just doesn't want to give up. Something like that. I will submit my board resignation with a copy to you as soon as I return to my office."

Twenty minutes later, he sat at his desk typing out his resignation letter. He placed it in an envelope and walked across campus to give it to Ellen Martin. She was surprised, reading his letter twice as he stood in front of her desk. She looked up at him. "I hate to see you leave the board, Mike. You have done a good job for us. I have to admit that, during our meetings, I often forgot that you are a new junior faculty member."

She smiled at him. "Your demeanor and especially your thoughtful analysis of our football problem seemed to be the words of someone with much more experience."

She read Mike's resignation one more time. "We will certainly miss you, but I completely understand Ed Johnson's decision." She stood and reached out to shake his hand. "Good luck."

He thanked her and walked out into the bright day. His mind was rapidly turning over as he processed what had just happened. He was a little surprised at himself. Despite board work left undone, he did feel a sense of relief. He certainly had some clarity. Now the rest of the board members must handle the football question.

25.

The traditional bonfire on Friday night before the first WKU home game was not as well attended as in recent years, but the few hundred supporters there loudly applauded the introductions of coaches and players. The team captain took the microphone for a few minutes to praise his teammates and to predict a rosy outcome of tomorrow's game. "Our first game was just a hiccup. Tomorrow, we are moving on to bigger things! Go Dogs!"

A large stack of burning logs illuminated cheerleaders who led the crowd with traditional yells for the Prairie Dogs. When one of cheers came to an end, there was an unplanned moment of nearly complete silence. Suddenly, a voice shouted out, "Fuck the Athletics Board! WKU football is the best!"

In response, several students took up the chant, "Fuck the Athletics Board! Fuck the Athletics Board! WKU football forever!" Suddenly, someone ran out of the shadows with a straw-stuffed dummy hanging from the end of a long pole. He held it over the fire, where it immediately ignited. Burning furiously, the flaming dummy swung around to reveal a crudely lettered sign on its chest. The reaction of the crowd was mixed. The loudest onlookers danced and laughed at the flaming effigy, while others turned their backs on the bonfire and the offensive sign and quickly walked away.

The next morning, Mike had just stepped out of the shower when his smartphone buzzed. It was Laura. "Good morning, Michael!"

Her cheery voice revived him. "Laura! Ahh! A friendly voice. Good Saturday morning to you!"

"Thanks, Michael. I'm certainly a friendly voice, but not so much of a happy voice. Did you go to the bonfire last night?"

"Nah. Just not in the mood for that stuff right now. Sleep was more important." He stifled a yawn then reached for his coffee maker.

She asked carefully, "Have you seen today's paper?"

"Not yet. I have tried to steer clear of the noise from the local media. From what I've heard from a few friends, many reporters didn't get it right—a lot of misinformation out there."

Laura became more serious. "Michael, I want you to look at the paper as soon as you hang up. And please—please don't even think about attending the game this afternoon."

Mike was a bit confused. "I don't understand. Sure, I'll read the paper.

It's still out on my doorstep. Can't you tell me? What—"

She interrupted, "Michael—just read the paper then call me back."

He put his phone down, slipped on his board shorts, and went to the front door to pick up his copy of the *Gazette*. He pulled off the rubber band and unrolled the paper to stare at a photo covering a good portion of the front page. It was the picture of last night's bonfire with a burning dummy hung high. The sign on the chest of the flaming figure read: "Professor Michael Wolf. Traitor."

Mike read a few words then angrily threw the paper on the floor. "Son of a bitch!" He walked noisily around his apartment, kicking the pages of the newspaper. He finally stood looking at himself in the mirror above the bathroom sink and spoke to his reflection, "Way to go, Mike! You are now famous—a famous asshole!"

Calming down, he called Laura back. She answered on the first ring. Mike's first words were "Wasn't that a nice photo! I think you're right. A game date is not a good idea—and, Laura, thanks for your support. Not too much of that around here lately."

He took a deep breath. "What we need is a hassle-free day. Let's escape to the county park just north of town. With the game going on, it should be quiet. The weather is good. I'll bring some drinks and dessert if you want to throw together some sandwiches."

"Good decision, Michael! I'll be ready in twenty minutes."

* * *

Mike spread a picnic blanket on one of the empty wooden tables that dotted the shaded park site. He and Laura were relaxed, enjoying each other's company in that peaceful place. The pleasant weather reflected the first days of fall, with temperatures just warm enough and a light breeze scattering a few falling leaves.

Mike opened a couple of beers. They drank silently, enjoying each other's company. She was wearing what she called her *week-end doing- nothing outfit*—a checkered blouse, shorts, and sandals. Her head was topped with straw hat to shade her face from the bright sun.

He matched her casualness with a WKU T-shirt, jeans, an old pair of running shoes, and a relic from his grad-school days—a beat-up U of I baseball cap.

Mike put his beer down and pulled out his smartphone to tune in to the football game that was just about to begin. He smiled at Laura's raised eyebrows. "Sorry, I guess I can't help myself. It's still hard to get WKU football out of my system."

The commentator described this first home game of the season with the pleasant weather and an excited crowd. He remarked on some empty seats in the stands—not a lot—maybe a thousand short of a sellout. He couldn't remember that ever happening.

Laura and Mike unwrapped their sandwiches while they listened. The game could be described as depressing, especially for Mike. The Prairie Dogs had been expected to defeat their opponents in a walkover. In the end, they barely won, 12-8. He turned off the radio by the time Coach Mitch Anderson was interviewed. If he had left it on, they would have heard Anderson once again blame the team's poor play on the distraction of the Athletics Board investigation.

Mike told Laura of his resignation from the board. Her reaction was one of relief. "Michael, it's a good thing. You are just too new at this professor business to be loaded down with heavy board responsibilities. I'm glad you are pulling away from that. And don't worry, you did a good job shaking up the old order."

"Honestly, I'm ready for a break. The piles of work on my desk at home and in my office have only gotten higher. I am at the point where I can't see the sink from the kitchen table—make that my *former* kitchen table. It's so jammed with books and papers that I take my most of my meals standing up."

She laughed at his description of his tasks undone. "I know what you mean. Even without the Athletics Board's machinations to worry about, I seem to have my own pile of stuff to do filling my desk. Sounds like we both need to get back to work!

"Michael, before we go, let's take a short walk to enjoy this park for a few minutes. I'll bet you will find it a nice break from the stresses of the board. I love to come here. There are so many interesting plants. Things you might miss at first glance." She stood, holding her hand out for his to stroll down a secluded path.

Laura shifted easily into her role as a biologist, telling Mike about the sometimes odd, but mostly beautiful, flora that defined the park. Mike couldn't help but notice how interested and knowledgeable she was in her work. He teased her, calling the specimens she showed him "that green and growing stuff."

Under the shade of a huge cottonwood tree, he stopped and pulled her into his arms. He looked into her laughing eyes and said, "You really need to teach me more about the ways of the wild weeds, Professor Biologist."

They kissed softly. She whispered, "That night together was so special—I love you, Michael."

Standing apart, Mike shook his head with a smile. "Dr. Sparks, here I am trying to learn a little bit about the nature around us, and you are stirring up"—he laughed—"my inner fires. I think I am losing it!"

Laura, feigning shock, stood back and shook her index finger in his face. "Why, Dr. Wolf, you . . . you . . . !"

Mike spoke in a mock formal tone, "Professor Sparks, in case you aren't aware of it, given the momentum of our relationship, I suspect that, in the future, hopefully, the *near* future, we will"—the next word would change their lives forever—"marry."

She fell back into his arms. "Michael, I do love you, and I want to spend my life with you, but . . ." She took deep breath. "Right now, there's a problem."

She pulled away from his embrace, brushing away her tears. He placed his hands on her shoulders. "Laura, what is it? Why are you crying?"

"Oh, Michael, I'm sorry to spoil this wonderful moment."

She stood away from him, holding his hands. "There is something that is going to get in our way—soon. I can't believe the timing. It's one of those happy-sad things for me . . . for us."

"I'm now a very confused guy, Laura. What's going on?

She took a deep breath. "Two of my colleagues at the University of Miami have just been awarded a large sea grant from NSF. I am part of the research team."

Laura put her hands to her face. The tears continued to fall as she spoke almost in a whisper, "It means I have to go to Florida to do my fieldwork. I haven't said anything to you because it was a long shot. None of us really thought we'd get it. But yesterday we got the news that the funding came through. Now I have to leave."

Mike put his arms around her shaking body. "Laura, it's OK. We have chosen this university business, and there is a lot that is expected of us. Don't worry . . . I'm not going anywhere." She pulled out a handkerchief to wipe her eyes. "You're right, we committed ourselves to this academic madness, and now we've got to do what we were hired for.

"This is a wonderful opportunity for me." She shook he head in consternation. "I'd almost given up hope on my proposal, then bang! The funding came though. There has been a lot of last-minute scrambling to cover classes."

Mike could sense the excitement in her voice as she told him about the project. "It is a chance for me to work with the best in the field *and* to spend a good deal of time at sea. Climate change has devastated much of the coral, and now that problem is being exacerbated by polluted runoff from coastal areas. The areas where we will sail are particularly vulnerable and—"

She stopped abruptly with an embarrassed smile. "Sorry, Michael, I guess you can tell that I am more than a little bit interested in the work."

"Laura, this is great! I'm excited for you. Don't worry about me. I can handle this. We will be in touch. What is it, a couple of weeks or so?" She looked down for a second, resting her chin on clasped hands.

"Michael, the field project will last until next June . . . at least. I will be involved in three research cruises and the analysis of much of my data in Miami." The tears were back as she said, "I won't come back here until next summer."

Mike was stunned by her news. He closed his eyes for a few moments as he absorbed her schedule. Then he gazed at her thoughtfully, realizing how much she had come to mean to him and how much it hurt him to see her cry. He reached over and wiped a tear from her cheek while trying to process her plans. "Listen to me, Dr. Sparks. We're adults living the academic life that we dreamed of and worked for—for a lot of years.

"Laura, I'm proud of you. Our education didn't prepare us for this—this sweet entanglement we have gotten ourselves into, but we will make it work. Go to Miami. Do your research." He smiled and winked at her. "We'll be OK."

Assistant Professor Laura Sparks left for Miami the following week.

26.

The morning after Laura's departure, Mike found himself missing her already. Not really hungry, he forced himself to eat a quick breakfast—any fuel in the tank would be helpful for the crammed day ahead.

He was on his way to the engineering building just before 7:00 a.m. It looked like another nice fall day ahead. The rising sun filtered through the yellowing leaves of the cottonwoods. Their shadows danced over the ground along his path.

He arrived at his office to find Jerry Larson standing outside the door, hands on his hips. Jerry was staring at the remnants of the thick glass panel where Mike's and his names had been prominently displayed with office hours and fall class schedules. Shards of glass were scattered across the floor. The smell emanating from the dark, wet substance mixed with broken glass was immediately identifiable. A rough sign taped to the side of the door read, "Hey, Wolf, you give shit to WKU football? We give you shit."

Jerry looked at Mike and shook his head. "Golly, Professor Football Fellow, I never imagined I'd be sharing an office with such a popular guy!"

Mike frowned. "I'll clean it up."

Jerry replied, "I suggest we call the campus cops. They'll want to see the mess and call the janitors."

Mike gave a sidelong look at his officemate and friend. "You really think that's necessary? The last thing I need is more attention."

"Yup, we've got to report this. Gotta cover your ass. These folks could get nastier."

Ten minutes later, a campus officer was questioning Jerry and Mike, while a custodian cleaned the glass and measured their window for a replacement. Jerry did most of the talking, while Mike, hands thrust in his pockets, stood to the side, quietly fuming about the damaged door. He knew he was the cause. When the officers finally left, he shook his head, speaking through clenched teeth. "Jerry, I'm really sorry about this. Those bastards! I'm taking a break to calm down. I'm useless here anyway."

He checked his watch. "I'll be back in forty-five minutes. I've got a lab coming up. If anybody shows up before then, just tell them . . . tell them to leave a message on my smartphone. Tell them whatever you want."

Jerry nodded. "Relax, Mike. Not to worry. It's too early in the semester for many visitors. I was putting together a report, but I agree, the mess on our door is a little too much for office work right now. Let's take a walk and get some fresh air."

There was little talk between them as they stepped out into the bright morning. They stopped for a few moments under an elm tree intent on shedding its foliage. Mike kicked at a pile of leaves on the sidewalk. "At least it's still a dependable season for falling leaves."

Jerry smiled at his friend's weak attempt to steer the conversation somewhere else. It didn't work. "Mike, I'm curious. It seems to me that this harangue over the state of WKU football isn't going away as quickly as you suggested a couple of days ago. That mess on our office door was serious."

Mike answered with a resigned sigh, "Jer, you're right. I am really sick of the negative reactions." Quickly his temper rose again. "And they are all over a frigging sport! Can you believe it? Is this a university or what? The more this goes on, the more I see football as a wart on the WKU's nose. It's not pretty.

"We are supposed do some serious stuff here, to teach students how to think, how to solve problems so they will ultimately be better than us, but"—he finished his sentence through clenched teeth—"but none of that applies to sacred goddamned football. That game is king, and all else be damned!

"If I had any doubts about the state of football when I gave that talk to the Athletics Board, I have none now. The more these negative reactions go on, the more I understand that the problem I discussed is just the tip of the goddamned iceberg!"

Jerry was glad they were in a quiet part of the campus. He stopped walking and put his hand on Mike's shoulder. "Mike, buddy! Slow down!

You don't have to convince me. I agree a hundred and ten percent. The question is what to do now. The other Athletic Board members must be processing the same data you are. And if I'm not mistaken, you are no longer on that board. Mike, it doesn't matter for you anymore. You have made your point. Let it go. They're smart. Let them wrestle with it."

Mike nervously pushed his wiry hair back over his forehead. He looked at his friend and spoke quietly, "Ignore my outburst, Jer. I agree. I'm just having a tough time letting all of this go, especially with the recent decoration on our office door."

His voice went up again, "Where is the president on this? She met with me before I left the board and said that there was going to be some serious follow-up. But I know through my contacts that no decisions have been made. The problems are absolutely crystal clear to me, and they should be to everyone else.

"Where is the dialogue? This university can't let this thing fester without some serious discussion, some constructive decisions. I have heard nothing. It's almost as if the leaders are saying, 'Let's not talk about the football problem, and maybe it will go away.' I really hope that's not true." Mike paused for a few seconds, looking down and shaking his head. "Ah, there I go again. Sorry you are on the receiving end of this, Jerry.

Believe me, I do want to let it go . . . . I'm working on it."

27.

T he days slipped away quickly as Mike attempted to concentrate on his teaching and research. Laura was on his mind, it seemed, almost all the time. She sent regular texts and emails to him describing her work in Florida. She was spending about equal time collecting samples at sea and doing some preliminary analysis in port. Mike could sense her excitement. Her messages made it clear that, despite her busy shore time in the lab, her favorite experiences were gathering samples on the cruises. She looked forward to synthesizing the results and writing some papers on her return. Her notes always ended with *Love, Laura*. He needed that. He really missed her.

Back at WKU, the local press had noted Mike's resignation from the Athletics Board. A couple of pundits called it a firing in response to the uproar after his presentation at the general faculty meeting last fall. Others accepted the board explanations that his resignation was due to his heavy academic load.

He stayed in contact with the acting board chair, Ellen Martin. She was not happy with the Athletics director, Tim Barnes, and the continuing bluster of the town representatives Ralph Bennett and John Roach. They had kept football as the central topic of the board meetings to counter the impact of Mike's analysis. It got to the point that their frequent interruptions began to impact on the board's ability to conduct business related to other sports.

One positive change was that Rory Kabat was now well enough to return as an active board participant. Ellen and Rory shared chair duties while he came back up to speed on the issues facing the board, especially the football troubles.

Out of concern over reports of the growing dysfunction of the board over the state of WKU football, President Summerville called a meeting with Kabat and Martin. She asked the two of them to form an ad hoc committee to deal specifically with the football problem. "I want to you to develop a way forward—out of this mess."

After a discussion of specific goals and a time line to complete the task, Kabat raised the question: "How about asking Mike Wolf for some help?" President Summerville said that she had already contacted Wolf's department chair, Ed Johnson, with the same suggestion. "Ed wasn't happy with my request, but after some negotiations over funding to hire a replacement to relieve Mike of some his course obligations, he relented.

Mike Wolf will join you.

"I want you to start next week. Give Rory your schedules so he can work out a convenient time for a weekly meeting. We have three weeks before you present your findings to the Athletics Board. They will review your work and advise me. I don't think we need to be reminded that this is a critical task. I wish we didn't have to do it, but we have no choice. Time is short."

That afternoon, Ed Johnson knocked on Mike's office door. Jerry was in class. Mike stood, reaching out to shake his chairman's hand. "Hi, Ed. What's the occasion?" He laughed. "I don't think I have screwed up lately, have I?"

Ed continued to stand. He shook his head at Mike's question. "No screwups, Assistant Professor Wolf, but I see that you have gotten into the Athletics Board's business again—despite all our discussions."

Mike was a little confused. "I don't quite follow."

"It seems that you are still a popular guy with our boss. She wants you back."

Mike cocked his head inquisitively. "Back? Back where? I'm not sure what you mean."

Johnson took a seat, looking around at Mike's cramped office, then back at Mike. "President Summerville and I have had a long talk about you and further board work. She wants to put you on a special subcommittee to work on WKU's"—he hesitated with a telling headshake—"WKU's ongoing football situation. I am not particularly happy with her request, but she certainly made a strong argument for your presence. The boss has spoken. You *will* be there.

"Next spring semester, you won't be teaching your sophomore class Introduction to Computer Engineering. Summerville has traded some budget with me so I can hire a substitute, and you can have release time for this subcommittee work.

"We will make it work. I trust your good judgment to squeeze those meetings in without interrupting the rest of your responsibilities."

Ed was silent for a few moments, considering the papers spread across Mike's desk. Then he looked at Mike. "I am still concerned about how your professional progress may be affected by this . . . this other work. I understand how the football situation has rocked the university on every level, and with your background and your explanation of the problem at the general faculty meeting, I certainly understand why you are needed. I hope that you and your cohorts can find a workable solution in a reasonable time. You need to get this thing off your back so you can focus your energy on your responsibilities in this department."

Mike nodded. "Thanks, Ed. I do hear you. I will keep things in perspective."

A few mornings later, Mike drove back to campus from a local high school where he met with a student advisor to discuss the preparation for university work in computer engineering. It was a pleasant exchange with no references whatsoever to WKU football. The meeting ended with an invitation to Mike to return to speak with interested students.

The rest of his day was full. He was scheduled for a brief conference with Ed Johnson followed by his first meeting with the president and the subcommittee on the football situation. He parked his car behind his apartment house for the short walk across campus to the engineering building.

Mike kept his head down, trying to avoid the dust being swept along the sidewalk by a gusty wind. When he stepped onto the narrow bridge over the creek a block from his destination, he was distracted by a few splashes in the water below. Somebody skipping rocks? He stopped just as small stone struck him in the chest. He brushed off the dirt and looked around. There was no one to be seen. Suddenly, a larger rock hit him in his bad leg, causing him to fall hard to his hands and knees. He saw a shadow of someone coming up behind him. Before he could rise, he was given a rough push into the creek. The water was a couple of feet deep, barely cushioning his fall. His bad leg took a beating.

Soaked, he got shakily to his feet, teetering on the rocky bottom of the stream. He took a couple of painful steps to rescue his briefcase, which had started to float away.

Wet and dirty, he crawled up the muddy bank to sit on the path and catch his breath. A sharp, stabbing pain shot up his right leg. He pulled out his smartphone and shook off a few drops of water. It still worked. He called Ed Johnson to reschedule their meeting then limped to the campus dispensary, gritting his teeth with each painful step.

Half an hour later, his scrapes were cleaned up. After an x-ray, the diagnosis was a sprained knee. The nurse had some sharp comments about Mike's vague explanation of his accident, but he felt that details of the attack would only bring in the campus police. He had no information about his attacker, and he just didn't want to deal with that right now.

He shuffled back to his apartment, wet and hurting. Angry thoughts filled his mind. *Just let me catch one of those sons of bitches. I' ll rip their goddamned heads off! Chicken-shit bastards won't even show their faces!*

After a quick shower and a change of clothes, he was ready to meet with the president and the newly formed Athletics Board subcommittee. Just before he left his apartment, he dug through his closet to pull out the cane he had used for several months after he broke his leg so long ago. He wasn't sure why he had kept it. He frowned as he dusted it off, thinking, *Here I go again.*

Mike moved slowly across campus, reacquainting himself with his old walking stick while he considered the attack he had just suffered. One of his students came down the path, giving him a wave. "Hey, Professor Wolf, how goes it?" He grinned. "You look pretty dapper with that cane." Then he laughed. "Maybe you should bring it to class to knock some computer sense into us!"

Mike shook his head and smiled. "You know, that might be a good idea." They stopped and chatted about class for a few minutes until his aching leg began to protest. "I have to get going, Jim. One of those infernal meetings awaits my presence."

A few minutes later, Rory Kabat, Ellen Martin, and Mike Wolf joined Jane Summerville in the conference room behind her office. After a brief welcome, she got down to business. "I remind you that we are here to consider the evidence that the WKU football program is not in line with the goals and standards of this university. If we agree with that evidence, the big question is, Can we fix it?

She paused for a second then added, "This is a big job, and we had better do it right. I will present our results at the January Athletics Board meeting. That gives us about three months. In the meantime, I ask that you do not speak to the press about our deliberations. If a reporter persists, send them to me. I suspect there will be a lot of starts and stops as we sift through the evidence, and we don't want to be premature with incorrect or partial information.

"One more thing. I want to make it clear that Mike Wolf has been invited to be a member of this group based on his clear statement of the problem. Also, I want everyone to know that because of his departmental responsibilities, his department chair has insisted that Mike's presence at these meetings be limited, which is to say that he will be included in our deliberations when I think that it is necessary. Otherwise, he will be available for contact from any of us by text, email, or telephone." Looking at Mike, she asked, "Did I miss anything?

He shook his head. "No problems. I am good with that." Mike was pleased to hear the limitations placed on his time in meetings while still being privy to the subcommittee's deliberations.

The president added, "Today, I have asked Professor Wolf to review the current situation so we are all starting at the same point."

The next forty-five minutes were tough for Mike due to the impact of his sad description on the sport he loved and the ache in his damnable leg. He gritted his teeth through the physical discomfort and reviewed the details of the cheating episode as well as applicable school and NCAA rules.

He concluded, "As you can see, the rules seem reasonable. The perpetrators have been dealt with. But we are not done with the problem. Now we must answer perhaps a more important lingering question, How do we get beyond this ugly incident with our significantly weakened football team? The three alternatives I laid out in my talk at the general faculty meeting for WKU's football future were (1) do nothing, (2) move to a lower NCAA division, (3) suspend the football program until we recover. Which course do we take?"

The room was silent for a few moments.

President Summerville shook her head. "This is a tough one. Any comments?"

Rory Kabat stood. Hands in his pockets and head down, he nervously walked back and forth along the edge of the conference table. He stopped and looked up at the president. "In all my experience with this university, I have never encountered such a problem. At times, I have found myself asking if we are still in control. He laughed ironically. "My experiences ducking gunshots on the battlefield seem pretty mild compared to this damnable football muddle.

"There are many other much more important concerns for the university at large—relevant academic programs, budget, acquiring up- to-date equipment, and hiring bright new faculty who will continue our tradition of relevance and excellence in education and research . . . but football?"

He shrugged his shoulders and sat down.

The president looked at Mike. "You were right in your board presentation, Dr. Wolf, there are the only three realistic solutions. And yes, their consequences have been staring at us in the face for quite a while. Any plan to weaken our football program will cause a firestorm from many, faculty, and students. And although no one wants to deal with the potential demise of WKU football., we must consider it as one of the possibilities." The president spoke as she began to place her papers in her briefcase. "Our next subcommittee meeting will be here same day and time next week. In the meantime, Mike, can you give us each a copy of your analysis in a confidential memo and send it around to all of us, say, by Monday? "I also remind you that our goal is to bring our conclusions and recommendations to the full Athletics Board for a discussion and a vote in two weeks."

28.

Outside the special Athletics Board subcommittee meetings, football problems continued to roil. The waning football season for the Prairie Dogs could only be described as lackluster. Their record of 5-6 placed them well down in league standings with no chance of making it to the playoffs. Coaches, current football players, many students, town supporters, and several media sports analysts continued to lay the main reason for lackluster season squarely in the lap of the Athletics Board—with many fingers pointed at Mike Wolf.

President Summerville attempted to set the press straight in a couple of interviews. She pointed to the *cause* of the problem—the organized cheating scheme by many football players. Her efforts didn't go far; the media only focused on the result of the problem—the poor WKU football record.

After the last game of the season, four of the best Prairie Dog players, three sophomores and one junior, decided to leave the university. This was not an easy decision for them. Upon transferring, they would have to sit out of football for a period as required by NCAA rules.

A month later, the departure of three more top players from the WKU was followed by the resignation of Assistant Coach Brady. The press, TV, and social media gave Brady and his rough, grating demeanor much attention. He didn't spare harsh words when speaking about the Athletics Board and, especially, Mike Wolf. "That academic jerk Wolf sabotaged the entire WKU football program."

His gravelly voice was heard over and over as his accusations were replayed on TV and online. When asked to explain the cheating by such a large group of players, his reply was "Goddammit! Were you guys born yesterday? College students cheat. Football players are no different. Why should they be singled out?"

A reporter challenged him, emphasizing the highly organized nature of the cheating scheme.

Brady responded loudly, "Bullshit! That is misinformation pushed by that asshole Wolf. Just another professor trying to make a name for himself!"

The Christmas holidays were a time for Mike to catch up. He took advantage of the quiet of the campus and his apartment to turn to the pile of coursework and unfinished research reports stacked on his desk and filling his computer files. Despite the break, concentration wasn't easy, especially when the reports of Brady's comment reached his ear.

He tried to ignore them to focus on his classes and research.

He was missing Laura, constantly checking his email for another note from her. She was extremely busy with her research, and he tried to keep his notes to her to a minimum, thinking, *For god's sake, Wolf, quit acting like a teenager. Get the hell back to work!*

The following January was unusually cold. The first Athletics Board meeting of the year got under way with board members removing heavy coats, hats, and scarves as they gathered around the conference table. Several pulled out handkerchiefs to wipe red and runny noses after treks across the snowy paths of the WKU campus.

This meeting had been called early, a full week before the semester began, and unusually, the president attended. She stood at the door as the members entered, handing to each attendee the draft response of the special committee on the cheating scandal.

After allowing a few minutes for the attendees to read the report, she immediately got to the point. "The impact of the football cheating debacle has gotten worse. Several football players and Athletics Department staff have left the university. There have been some violent reactions—some resulting in injuries."

She looked sternly at the group. "We have some important work to do to clean up this mess."

The somber faces around the table indicated silent agreement with her assessment.

As she began to speak again, Ralph Bennett, one of the local businessmen, interrupted her. "I'm surprised that you don't seem to recognize that the cheating debacle, as you call it, has been blown out of proportion by that idiot Wolf! I am glad to see him off the board."

Not responding immediately, Summerville gave Bennett a few seconds to reconsider the insults he had just thrown across the table. He was silent. Coach Anderson spoke up, "Ralph, that was uncalled for. We are here because we have a problem *now*. We must solve it *now*. Throwing rocks at each other will get us nowhere."

Bennett was flustered. This wasn't the WKU football program he had supported for so many years. He suddenly stood, sneering at the head of the table. "You academics know nothing."

He left the room without another word.

Jane Summerville placed her hands on the table, looking around at the group and shaking her head slowly. "That was too bad—I will call him after we finish here. In the meantime, there is some important work to do. "Last semester, I established a special committee to dissect this football issue—to recommend steps to deal with the problem. Their recommendations are in front of you. I have dropped into your meeting to emphasize the importance of the job they have done and to encourage you to consider each of their recommendations carefully."

She stood, thanked the board, and left the room, turning the meeting over to Rory Kabat.

Rory reached across the conference table and turned on a computer projector. The short list of team violations was displayed prominently on a screen at the end of the conference table.

> **Infractions**
>
> Twenty-six players conspired to alter grades to maintain their eligibility.
> Grade modifications were facilitated by number of students who worked in the computer center and were paid by the football players.
> An Athletics Board member was physically attacked for his analysis of the cheating incident.

Kabat pointed to the screen. "I don't think that there is any doubt that these actions violate the basic principles of WKU—honesty and fairness.

"We are convinced that these offenses reflect a deep-seated problem among the current WKU football team. Based on the evidence, we strongly recommend the following."

He brought up another display.

> **Proposed Actions**
> Immediately suspend football activity at WKU for two years.
> After two years, restart the program at a lower NCAA division (no scholarships).

"I invite comments and suggestions for any revisions of these actions." Ralph Bennett's angry voice lashed out., "What in the hell is this?

Call a two-year moratorium on WKU football? You can't even think about doing that!"

John Roach was incredulous. "Consider leaving the top NCAA division? No scholarships? You are pulling the rug out from under the Prairie Dogs! This is wrong! Bad management!"

His shouting was brought to a quick end by a loud retort by Rory Kabat. "I absolutely disagree with this outburst!" He paused, looking around the table. "We've seen our team pulled down by—by outright criminal activity. It's not just one or a few players. It's many.

"Another part of this problem is that there is a group outside the university that has infected our program with promises of money to athletes and, lately, with violence. They must be clearly identified and punished under current laws."

Nodding to Mike Wolf, he went on, "Given the nasty words floating around and the physical threats to this courageous board member, we can only conclude that a serious honesty problem has infected our current football program."

Rory pounded his fist on the table. "I ask you, are we a university with a football team? Or is this an independent football team connected to WKU simply for convenience?"

He looked around the table, making eye contact with each board member. "Are there innocent players? You bet! But many of them have been silent when the identification of the culprits has been so important. As far as I am concerned, those players who looked the other way are guilty by association. If the team disappears, they will know it was their fault too."

Rory took his seat. Remarks across the table became more cacophony than discussion.

Kabat glared angrily at the sources of the loud comments. He brought the noise to an end with a bang of his gavel and a well-delivered order: "Stop!"

Roach and Bennett stood abruptly. They jammed papers into their briefcases, refusing to make eye contact with anyone. The council room was suddenly eerily silent. Finally, Tim Barnes rose and sternly addressed the board chair, "Professor Kabat, I cannot believe that you would allow this unwarranted course of action. I am greatly disappointed in your leadership."

Kabat thoughtfully glanced at his notes. After a few seconds, he looked up and responded sharply, "I have been in too many firefights to give your comments much credence, Director Barnes."

Pointing to the screen, he added, "If you bothered to read what is written up there, you would have noticed that the word *proposed* is clearly attached to the word *actions*. That can't be much clearer. We are here to discuss these, modifying them where necessary before we give our final recommendations to the president and the academic senate."

Kabat pounded his fist on the table, raising his voice. "No final decisions have been made. Your behavior is unwarranted, especially for a person in a leadership position."

Rory paused, exasperation showing on his face. "Please feel free to start the conversation by asking us to explain—again—how we came up with this"—he articulated the next word slowly and clearly—"proposal."

Barnes hesitated at the door and looked down for a moment. Ralph Bennett put his hand on the Athletics director's shoulder. "C'mon, let's get out of here."

Barnes turned to Bennett. "I have to admit that our chairman makes a good point. No final decisions have been made. Let's sit down and ask some questions. I know there is a better plan."

Bennett shook his head and spoke loudly over Barnes's shoulder. "These idiots are destroying more than sixty years of WKU football. I'm not going to be part of it." He turned and walked out of the auditorium. Tim Barnes took a deep breath and went back to the conference table.

29.

When spring football practice got underway the next April, a decision had not yet been made about WKU football, but the potential for the suspension of the sport was still alive, and it cast a shadow over the team. Eighty-five players had been expected to attend spring practice—only forty-five showed up.

At the end of the first day of practice, reporters from the *Gazette* and the local television station waited at the edge of the practice field for Coach Anderson to dismiss the players for the afternoon.

Anderson finally sent the team to the locker room and walked over to the newspeople. He appeared to be his old self, relaxed and smiling and giving friendly nods to several reporters he knew personally. The reporters' questions revolved around the decrease in the size of the team roster. Anderson's response was short and to the point. He laid the blame on the Athletics Board's response to the cheating incident.

"I don't support cheating in any way, whether on the field or in the classroom. Unfortunately, the Athletic Board's approach to this problem seems to be overkill. It is a threat to the future of WKU football. I know that final decisions have not been made yet, but some proposals have already caused plenty of worry among the players and the coaches."

Anderson paused, wearily rubbing his face with both hands. "Sorry, I'm a little tired. It's been a long day."

Mac Ellis, a *Gazette* reporter, pressed Anderson for more information. "Coach, can you give us some details about the fall-out from the board investigation? What do you think the long-term impact will be?"

He hesitated, not wanting to rehash the problem. He was tired; spring practice needed his attention. He looked back at the reporter and said, "I'm not sure what the report has in store for us, but there have already been some negative impacts."

He turned to walk back to the locker room. The persistent reporter followed him. "What negative impacts?"

Anderson stopped. With his hands on his hips, he looked down for a moment and took a deep breath. He wanted to get into the locker room, but he knew he had to deal with these questions sooner or later; otherwise the press would get it wrong.

He turned back to face the reporter. "You already are aware of most of these. We had a lousy season last fall, we have lost some of our best players and an assistant coach, and there have been fewer new recruits this season. And to top it off, we have lost some local sponsor support—not a pretty picture."

Forcing a smile, Anderson attempted to be positive about the future. "There is no question that the situation will be tough for a while, but we have some good new talent." He gave a weak smile. "Not to worry, the Prairie Dogs will rise again."

He gave the reporters a half-hearted wave and walked away.

The WKU Alumni organization had expressed a similar optimistic outlook, but it became tempered in the passing months. There had also been an unexpected development in WKU student attitudes. The campus newspaper, the *WKU Viewpoint*, surveyed student opinions about the future of football at the university. Compared to past surveys, the response to this one was huge. The WKU student population of a little over 15,000 students produced 7,276 replies. No past campus survey had ever produced more than 1,000 responses. The results shook the university community—53 percent of the respondents favored dropping the sport.

In the meantime, Mike tried to put thoughts of football aside to recover what he called his *engineering professor attitude*. That focus was interrupted when he received a strange email on one April morning. It was a single sentence: *You are going to pay, Wolf.*

He shared it with his officemate. "Look at this thing, Jerry. I can't really make heads or tails out of it."

Jerry's inhaled sharply as he read it. He didn't hesitate. "Given all the football crap you've been through, I'd say that is downright threatening, Mike. You have been attacked once already. Call the cops."

"What can the cops do? The source of the email is a café downtown.

We couldn't find the person who sent it if we wanted to."

Jerry was insistent. "Believe me, Mike! Somebody out there wants to kick your butt!"

Mike laughed. "Let 'em come. They've never dealt with a pissed-off Mike Wolf before. And believe me, I'm getting to that pissed-off point. I'm ready to kick some butt myself!"

Jerry held up his hands. "Whoa, Captain Marvel! I didn't realize who I was dealing with. Pity the idiot who takes you on!"

Then he got serious. "Mike, I know you are sick of all this football baloney that is still flying around, but you better be careful where you tread. There could be something to those threats."

Later that day, Jerry's warning became a reality. Mike left his apartment to pick up something for dinner. He walked through a familiar alley on his way to his favorite pizza parlor when he was confronted by four individuals holding clubs.

Two of them grabbed him and dragged him into a window-less portion of an alley darkened by the lengthening afternoon shadows. They pushed him up against a wall and proceeded to beat him. Mike didn't go quietly. He fought back with everything he had. He bloodied one guy's nose only to be hit by more fists and a glancing blow with a two-by-four. Although he was severely beaten, he didn't let the perpetrators get away clean. He used his cane to skewer one of them in the ribs and hit another on his head so hard that the attacker collapsed. The other three were closing in when the wail of a police siren caused them to scatter. They quickly faded into the darkness.

The police found Mike bloodied, leaning against a brick wall with a man unconscious at his feet.

30.

The nurse sitting beside the bed noticed her patient was awake. He struggled to make sense out of the constriction to his right arm and the difficulty in moving his head. She laid her hand gently on his left arm and spoke quietly, "Hi, Mr. Wolf. You are OK. Beat up a bit but already on the mend. Just take it easy. Your head will clear as you come out of the anesthesia."

Mike gradually became more alert—aware of bandages that covered one eye, his nose, and his mouth. He attempted to reach up and touch his face. It wasn't easy. His right arm was in a cast, and his left hand was heavily bandaged. He muttered, "Where am I? What happened?"

"I was told that you were attacked a few blocks from the university. Do you remember any of that?"

Mike thought for a minute then shook his head. "I can't remember where I was or what I was doing." He paused as a light seemed to go on inside his bandaged head. "I was home, in my apartment. I stepped outside to get something to eat and . . . I'm not sure."

"Don't worry. In a situation like this, details often return slowly. For now, just relax. I am going to change a couple of bandages to make you more comfortable and make it easier for you to speak.

"After that, you'll see the doctor. If he feels you are up to it, the police and a professor from the university are waiting to see you. Your university friend has been sitting in the waiting room for nearly six hours."

Mike smiled. *Good old Jerry.*

A half hour later, his head was clearer, and his new bandages made it easier for him to move. He could flex his very sore hands and lightly touch the stitches on his nose and his forehead. There were even a couple on his lower lip. He shook his head, thinking, *God, what a mess!*

Two policemen were ushered in, one from the city and a WKU security officer. In the next twenty minutes, Mike related to them all the details of the incident he could remember. "I know I tried to defend myself with my walking stick at one point."

Mike paused and shook his head. "Everything got kind of fuzzy after I was down. I can't really remember what happened next. Do you know any details?"

He received a description of the attack based on the testimonies of two witnesses who had called the police. One officer said, "When we arrived, you and the guy you clobbered were both on the ground about five feet apart. He is currently in another room of this hospital—with a guard at his door."

Mike's face lit up. "Finally got one! Who is he?"

"He isn't talking yet, and he carried no ID. In my experience, it is just a waiting game until he realizes that he got caught while his buddies got away." He smiled. "Don't worry. We are patient. We will get them all sooner or later."

The police officers stood to leave. "We had better go—paperwork to do. Don't be surprised if we knock on your door again. Heal well, Professor Wolf."

When the officers left, the nurse returned to advise Mike that he had another visitor, if he wasn't too tired from the last group. Mike smiled weakly at the nurse. "What I really need is a nap. But sure, send him in."

The nurse corrected him. "It's not a him. It's a her." She stepped aside to reveal Laura standing in the doorway. She flew into his room and stood awkwardly next to his bed—wanting to touch him but afraid to, with all his bandages. Her tears were unstoppable.

"Michael, I heard from Jana Wood, my officemate at WKU. She texted me in Miami . . . What did they do to you?"

She could see his wide smile despite the bandages on his face. "Laura! You are here!" He reached out with his scratched and bruised hand to touch hers. She bent down and gently kissed his fingers.

He whispered, "Not to worry, my sweet Laura. It's not as bad as it looks, and you are just the medicine I need!"

He pressed her hand lightly to his bruised lips.

She wiped the tears away and smiled at him. "Michael, I have a surprise for you." He opened his eyes widely with a curious muffled "Yes?"

"My time in Florida was to be another three weeks, but that has changed. I'm home for good. I want to keep an eye on my football fellow." She laughed. "To make sure he stays out of trouble."

"But, Laura, you have research to finish, and I'm going to be stuck in rehab for a few weeks. I'd like to be healed a bit more so"— he laughed—"I can get these stupid bandages off." He gave another muffled laugh. "And I can get my hands on you!"

Laura covered a smile halfway between delight with Mike's words and embarrassment that someone might be listening. "Michael . . . oh, Michael, I love you so much."

She paused, taking a deep breath. "Here is the situation. I'm through with gathering samples. I only have about three weeks of work to do in the laboratory, and it can be done either there or here. After I got word of your injury, I spoke with my boss and proposed that I return early. She OK'd it. My colleagues in Miami are packing up all my material as we speak.

"So, Mr. Ex-Football Guy, you've got me"—she touched his hand—"in more ways than one."

A few days later, a report of the attack on Mike Wolf was headlined in the local *Argyle Record*. The individual captured by Mike was the break authorities were looking for. Questioning by the police revealed that he was a nonstudent hired by the same collection of individuals who were at the heart of the football cheating conspiracy. He admitted that he and three others were instructed specifically to harass Wolf to the point that he would back off his criticism of the football program and separate himself from any Athletics Board business. They picked the wrong guy.

At the end of the semester, the Athletics Board recommended that WKU should discontinue intercollegiate football immediately with a goal of restarting the football program after a two-year cooling-off period. That recommendation moved through the university bureaucracy in record time. There were many unhappy players and fans, but surprisingly, there were no organized protests.

EPILOGUE

Mike walked across the campus toward his office. His old measures of the passing years were visible in the distance. Even with the arrival of another fall, the trees around Tower Hall were now so tall that that landmark was nearly hidden from sight.

A cane was now Mike's permanent companion for any treks longer than a block—an aftermath of the violence during the uproarious days following the football cheating scandal so many years ago. He didn't want to believe that he needed a walking stick, but a couple of near falls had made their point. His sense of humor, as usual, got him past those incidents. He smiled, thinking, *Ahhh, Dr. Tripod experiences the fortunes of age!*

Mike was now a full professor and recently elected assistant department chairman. Teaching and research were still his primary focus, but he knew that situation would only last another year or so. Ed Johnson was talking more about what he would be doing in retirement. It was clear to the rest of the faculty that Mike would be his successor.

Halfway to the engineering building, Mike glanced at his watch. Early for his morning appointments, he decided to detour to Arnold Stadium to sit for a few minutes. He did this once or twice a week when the weather cooperated.

Taking a seat high up in the stadium overlooking the fifty-yard line, he looked around, reflecting on the fact that the only football games that occurred on this field in the last few years were intermural competitions between fraternities and other campus clubs.

WKU had discontinued its participation in intercollegiate football nearly five years ago. The road to dropping the sport had started five years before that when Mike gave his speech to the faculty criticizing the then unacceptable state of the sport. Football had limped along for another few years, but the downward momentum was too much. Losing seasons became the rule. Student interest and ticket sales waned as more players left the team and the school. Numbers of new freshman players and JC transfers became a trickle. A half-full stadium for home games was not unusual.

Sportswriters and commentators were brutal when the Prairie Dogs were beaten, often badly, game after game. Mitch Anderson, the head coach, finally resigned. He had been offered a position at a university on the West Coast.

Scrambling by the Athletics Department to fill Anderson's shoes brought in a promising replacement from a small Midwestern college. Director Barnes remained positive that the football situation would improve.

It did not. In fact, it got worse.

At the time, many news pundits gave up on the program, suggesting that WKU drop football completely.

And that was what happened—WKU did not field a football team. Barnes attempted to assure former supporters that "this is just a hiccough in the history of fine WKU football. We will be back." His remarks fell on deaf ears. Football was gone forever.

Mike had mixed feelings when that sport disappeared from the grass of Arnold Stadium. His conflicted love-hate relationship still persisted.

A sad event related to WKU's glorious football past was the death of Tank Kozlowski. He was found dead one fall afternoon, lying peacefully on his pile of raked leaves. Only a handful of people showed up for a brief memorial: Dr. Morgan, Tim Barnes, Ellen Martin, Mike, and one of the women who cooked at Tank's home. The disappearance of football at WKU took on another meaning when Tank's ashes were spread across WKU's old football field—just below the stands where Mike now sat. He processed those memories for what seemed to be the millionth time.

It had been a long while between his good player / poor student days and his emergence as a talented engineering professor and Athletics Board member who confronted a football cheating scandal. The years following saw sporadic national movement toward cleaning up college football. At one university, football players attempted to unionize. The courts threw that effort out, ruling that college football was a sport, not subject to unionization. It was obvious to Mike that the judges who made that quick decision did not understand the complexity and the problems of modern college football.

Despite a tremendous national reaction to the WKU football scandal, those who had a platform from which they could pressure all college football, not just WKU, to clean up its act failed to follow through. The topic was left in limbo. Certainly, a few schools used the WKU incident as an incentive to examine their own programs. But after a few years, most of those investigations yielded insignificant results—mainly empty promises to fix the sport. Radical changes were limited to a handful of smaller, lower division schools with some, as WKU, dropping the sport.

Mike understood that American football was a tradition that had developed as the country did. In its unique way, it reflected many American characteristics, including the physical toughness that personifies Americans in the face of difficulty, no matter the ramifications. He still hoped that one day the football tradition would resume at WKU.

He glanced around Arnold Stadium. It was still a busy place for sports such as soccer and track-and-field with their own loud and appreciative spectators, but those events never came close to filling the arena—never paid for its upkeep as football had in the past. While the infield grass and the surrounding track were still in good shape, the huge empty stadium had a gray look—weathered wooden seats with cracks and splinters and rusted metal supports. The ubiquitous ads that had decorated the walls of the stadium during the peak of WKU football were gone or torn and faded, hardly readable.

Rays of the bright rising sun touched the top of the stadium. Mike's thoughts came back to the present as he squinted into the sunlight. Time to head to the office. He stood stiffly, suddenly becoming aware of someone standing behind him.

He turned to see Laura, on her way to her own classes. "Hi, Michael. I thought I might find you here, analyzing the worries of the university."

"Laura! Sorry I ran off without saying goodbye, but you seemed pretty involved with your computer, and our boy, Mikey, was still asleep. I thought you could use some quiet time."

"A good decision, my favorite husband. Yes, I did take advantage of Mikey's desire to doze a bit longer. He did, and I got a lot done."

Laura sat down close to Mike, setting her bags on the bench.

"Yes, our Mikey is quite a guy. I think we made a pretty good son."

Mike put an arm around her shoulders. "We sure have come a long way since I dumped my breakfast in your lap."

Laughing, she sat closer. "Ah yes! Our now famous breakfast incident!

That is one for our family history book!"

She squeezed his hand. "FYI, your son is now holding forth with his second-grade class, his mom is about to give a lecture to her freshman biology class, and his dad . . . hmm . . . his dad is sitting here in this former football stadium staring at . . . at the grass or something."

Mike chuckled. "You do know my ways! This is my morning Zen period before I meet those future engineers wanting to impress me with their lab projects. They are writing some software to control some small drones. Something for agricultural applications. They'll test them on Friday. I hope they don't kill themselves—or me!" He leaned over to give Laura a kiss.

"Oh, my handsome engineer, that's really not so scary. If you want fright, just come visit one of my freshman biology labs."

Mike looked at Laura with laughter in his eyes. "Tell me, sweet Laura, is it really true that our son looks exactly like me?"

Laura rubbed her chin thoughtfully. "Let's see. He has curly hair and he is athletic. Yeah, he just might favor his father—a bit."

Then she added, nudging Mike in the ribs, "But certainly he'll be taller and better looking! And you know, he does ask an awful lot of questions about stuff biological. In fact, just the other day, he gave me a short lecture on earthworms. Very well organized!"

Laura looked thoughtfully at the rays of the sun now pouring across the top of the stadium. "Michael, this is a wonderful time—bringing up Mikey in the shadow of this university. It's so special."

Squeezing Mike's hand, her eyes glistened as she said, "The next few years will certainly be interesting. For some reason, I think there will be days when Mikey and his dad will sit together in this old stadium, contemplating the world, talking about engineering."

Mike nudged Laura. "How about biological engineering?" She leaned over and gave him a kiss on the cheek.

Laura paused for a second, looking down at their clasped hands. "Michael, there is something else that has just come up about our son. I wasn't sure how to tell you this, but . . ." She closed her eyes.

"Yesterday, Mikey came home from school with . . . with a football under his arm."

End